MW01386168

l

June 5/16

Walking Mary Home

When Love and Cancer Collide

Bert C. Michel

Prodigal Press
http://www.prodigalpress.com

ISBN: 0989702006
ISBN-13: 978-0-9897020-0-3

Praise for Walking Mary Home

Cancer can't kill a real love story; it deepens it and eventually immortalizes it--Bert and Mary have proved that love never fails. Although this is a story about the rude interruption the last enemy imposes on life, what can't be ruined gets even stronger. If you read this book you get the privilege of tagging along on one of the great love stories. Bert undresses the deep emotions of the unthinkable--a love story suddenly cut short. Bert and Mary will pick up where they left off someday, and it will be glorious. In the meantime, the memories of a walk that was for keeps will have to do. Mary and Bert lived and walked and made God glad by their marriage. Do your heart and all in your life a favour--drink deeply from this story and then love generously while you can.

Pastor Rick Baker
Calvary Baptist Church
Oshawa, Ontario

My former student and friend, Bert Michel, has served us all well by writing this compelling account of his painful journey with his beloved Mary during their battle with her cancer. The book is candid, insightful, and hopeful, and it will enrich the lives of others caught in the same battle. But it's not just for people dealing with cancer or other terminal illnesses, because one of the major contributions of the book is its demonstration that couples manage the dying process well only if they have lived together well along the way. And Bert clearly shows that all of this is ultimately because of the grace of God, who is the hero of the story. The narrative itself is instructive at multiple levels, but the inclusion of questions for reflection multiplies the value of the book for personal growth or even group studies. This book is both an illustration and means of God's redemptive work in this broken world.

Every blessing, Stan.

Dr. Stanley K. Fowler
Professor of Theological Studies
Heritage Theological Seminary
Cambridge, Ontario

I had the privilege of editing *Walking Mary Home*, and it was just that—a privilege. With a mother who is battling brain cancer, and two in-laws fighting blood and breast cancer, this book hits close to home for me. I've never read anything so honest about cancer or about love. It is a rare glimpse into the exquisite beauty that is marriage, and the loss that is death, and how faith in Christ can reconcile the tension between love and loss. I highly recommend Walking Mary Home to anyone desiring to know some unexpected truths about cancer and chemotherapy. But I especially recommend the book because it is a witness to the fact that joy can be found even in walking a loved one home.

Emily T. Wierenga
Award-Winning Journalist, Blogger,
Commissioned Artist, Speaker and Author of
Save My Children, *Chasing Silhouettes* and
Mom in the Mirror.

"But, Bert, I can't eat one more spoonful of Jell-O," Mary rasped as Bert sat on her hospital bed which was clearly out of place in their living room, coaxing his beloved to sustain her body just a little longer.

I had the privilege of visiting with Bert, Mary and their family for a few days, just before Mary was admitted to hospital for the final time. I have never been so freely invited to share the intimacy of two soul-mates as in those hours. As far as I could tell, Bert and Mary held back nothing from each other, from their children and from their closest friends. We talked when Mary had strength, kept respectful silence when she dozed, laughed at memories and always prayed – both silently and sometimes together. Those hours are etched in my heart as hallowed glimpses of hard-won love.

"Mary, I'll eat half if you eat the other," Bert enticed Mary. It had worked the last time and there was a small rise in energy when she did. But the look on Mary's face as she witnessed her husband forcing the dessert into his mouth told me she was just too exhausted.

"Bert, you'll be wearing the rest of the Jell-O in your ear if you keep this up," I interjected before he could think of another strategy to lure Mary to eat something, anything. Mary turned to me with thankful relief.

Sara, their daughter, looked me straight in the eye and half-commanded, "Dad needs a break. Why don't you take him to the Sunday night concert at church tonight, Len? If you leave now, you will be just in time."

I knew Mary needed rest. I also knew Bert didn't want to miss even one second with Mary. But he could use some care and Mary's nod confirmed I needed to act. "Let's go Bert. It will do you good." Bert reluctantly agreed. I think we were meant to spend some time together as we went to that concert. We were gone within minutes.

What do you say to a man who desperately wants to relieve his wife's suffering but who cannot give up hope she will recover? As we journeyed together that evening, Bert talked about how much he missed church over the past couple of weeks, his job, what sustained him in the darkest hours, where Sara might buy her first house, and the lift that the music that night gave him.

I waited for the opportunity to tell him that he would need to tell Mary that it was okay if she couldn't keep walking with him in this world, and give her permission to go. I know he didn't want to hear that and it bankrupted my inner resources to say what was clearly true to my best friend. I blurted it out the best I could. And Bert listened and understood.

You are about to enter into a similar journey with Bert, as he shares with you the sacred story of walking his wife home. It can't be easy to let others into your most painful story without varnishing, embellishing, concealing or posing but Bert keeps this story real. I know Bert, and his voice doesn't get distorted by a word processor.

I can vouch for the veracity of the story. Listen up, my friend. This is a tale worth hearing. It will awaken your desire to walk with God and with the ones He has called you to love.

Len Thompson
Founding Director of Urban Sanctuary, a center for Evangelical spiritual formation in Edmonton
He holds a degree in theology and a Masters in counselling (Doctor of Ministries degree in progress). Len teaches at Taylor Seminary in

Edmonton and at Rocky Mountain College in Calgary. He and Bert have been ministry and personal friends since 1982.

TABLE OF CONTENTS

To Mary ~ As a wife and friend you were supreme. Your love was deep and steady. It shaped your life. It formed my life too. I write so that a beautiful love may be remembered. Walking with you made my life rich.

Through our cancer journey, walking with you made me admire you. You always remained my lover. You also became my heroine.

And to our Lord ~ Mary's love was a human reflection of Yours, one of Your beautiful gifts to me and to our world. Now she knows the highest love. I give my sincere praise and gratitude to You. Thank You so much for the gift of Mary.

PREFACE

It was evening, the day before Mary's funeral. I was sitting at my desk, thinking and praying. I had told our pastor and children that I wanted to say some things at the funeral. I felt I needed to share how blessed I'd been to know Mary and live with her, and to walk with her through most of our lives.

Mary and I were married when we were only twenty years old, and it would have been our 38th anniversary just eight days after she died. I had learned so much with and from her. The longer I sat the more I wanted to say. I began to jot down some of my thoughts as memories played on one another.

I wanted to say many things about the treasure of our love. We were one of those couples that truly learned to love one another. My mind strayed all the way back to our wedding vows, those promises I made without even beginning to know what they meant. I reflected on how we had lived out those vows. We held to each other from that day forward, through sickness and health, through great times and hard, through poorer and richer, and as we did, we learned to deeply love each other.

For us, real love succeeded the vows. Of course we both thought it was love before. But to be honest, at best it was like a seed of love. It would be our living that led to the loving. There was so much I wanted to say about that love, and how it was no lucky accident.

And then the whole cancer journey played through my mind. There were so many things Mary and I learned about cancer, so many things I wished we had known years ago. I wanted to talk about those things, but I found myself getting confused. I didn't even know where to begin to talk about cancer. I just knew I wanted to. Or rather, needed to.

Reflecting on the cancer journey made me want to say even more about Mary. Her quiet courage, faith, and strength were so evident. As I walked the road of cancer with her I was awed by who she became. I was so proud of her. I wanted to publicly thank God for things He taught us through that cancer journey. I wanted to thank God for what He had done in Mary. I wanted to talk about loving someone even more than you used to, because of cancer.

Reflecting on love, cancer and Mary's spiritual journey made me want to talk about God. Because the things that matter most in our walk with God are not learned sitting in pews or putting pen to paper, are they?

They are learned so much more deeply when life and love are stretched to the breaking point, when clinging to God is all you can do, when you don't even know what to pray anymore, but you know you need to pray. And as you pray, sometimes all you can do is weep before Him. As you let it happen, a story is written on your heart, in ways you never knew existed. It's a story for which words seem inadequate. Oh how I wanted to find words to share some of that story.

As I sat there, an hour passed, then another. I realized I couldn't even begin to say the things I wanted to. It was too much. I simply didn't feel adequate. I couldn't come up with the words I needed. So time being the tyrant it is, I did what I had to do. I isolated a few thoughts, printed them to read to people the next day, and got ready to sleep.

Sometimes thoughts become more focused for me as I sleep. They did that night. I woke up and knew I had to write things down. I didn't want to lose anything I had been thinking about the day before. I wanted to keep memories of walking with Mary alive. I wanted to clarify the love lessons and the cancer-lessons, and especially the God lessons. I wanted to go further into the God story I had been living. I knew if I didn't begin soon, memories would gradually fade.

I want to write as if I am sitting next to you, engaged in a quiet conversation about the love of my life, and my experience of walking her home when our love and her cancer came into collision.

Though I will share some of my thoughts about cancer, I am not a doctor. So nothing I write is intended to replace the advice of a medical practitioner.[1] It's just us, our story.

We walked together through life. We walked through cancer. And then we walked a final mile. She is home now. It was my great privilege to walk her there.

---

[1] Names and genders and places, especially those of doctors, have frequently been changed.

1. A Walk Worth Writing About

Our love grew to be a beautiful love.

It started very small, but in time and with nurture, it grew until it was beautiful.

I remember something that happened early in the cancer journey. One of Mary's sisters, Nancy, was asking her friend at church to pray for us. The friend asked if she had ever met us. Nancy mentioned that Mary and I had attended their church the previous Sunday along with others of the extended family. As Nancy described us to her friend, she exclaimed, "Oh, is that the couple that loves one another so much?"

I guess she had seen us holding hands as we crossed the parking lot, and as we stood to sing in worship. Perhaps she had seen the way we talked with one another, or Mary sliding close to me as we settled in for the message at Cobourg Alliance Church. None of those things had been put-on or an act of any kind. It's just who we were.

We used to get interesting reactions on our street. We were in the habit of walking together, and it was always hand-in-hand. The neighbors would often wave, and sometimes roll down their window to chat as they were driving past. One neighbor who frequently stopped to talk usually greeted us with, "Well, how are the two love-birds today?"

Our next-door neighbor once told me that when we first moved on to the street and he saw us walking he assumed we must be newly-weds. As he put it to me, "I thought you guys were second-timers."

A Comfortable Kind of Love

We simply enjoyed being with each other. We were rarely apart, because we never wanted to be. Our preference was almost always to be together. Sure, I did some guy things and she did some girl things. But doing things apart was the exception, not the norm. Within a short time of being apart, we wanted nothing more than to be together again.

Twice in our married life, we separated for more than a week. The first time, I went with a group of men to do a church-raising in British Columbia. We were apart for two long weeks. By the first night I missed her badly. The second week, I missed her so much I could close my eyes and distinctly see her face. I mean, literally see it.

As our man-group approached Oshawa on our way home, I was so excited I was almost giddy. I couldn't understand why the other guys didn't seem as overjoyed to see their wives again. I was in the back seat, on the driver's side for the last leg of the journey. I hated being there as we turned the last corner for Merv's house. I knew Mary was there waiting for me. I couldn't see her around the headrests and the other guys. I remember the strong feeling of nothing on earth mattering to me more than seeing her right at that moment.

The other extended time apart was when Mary went with some of her siblings to the Netherlands because her dad's regiment in the underground resistance was being honored fifty years after World War II. This time we were apart for three weeks.

It was the longest three weeks of my life. I couldn't stand still as I waited for her to come through the doors at Pearson Airport. We finally saw each other, and she ducked under the ropes, dropped her bags and came running to me. We embraced each other and immediately found each other's lips for one of those timeless kisses that go from hungry, to happy, to passionate, to gentle, then back again. We might still have been there if not for a rude interruption by one of the sisters. As if it really was enough, already!

Our love grew passionate but also very comfortable. Like most couples, we learned early in our marriage that we could push the wrong buttons and make each other anything but comfortable. But after a few of those dust-ups we decided we'd sooner not do life that way. Instead of the wrong buttons, we'd try to push the right ones, doing things that make each other feel welcome and wanted and loved. We both did that, and our love became comfortable in the best sense of the word. Not a "take-each-other-for-granted" comfortable, but, "I love being with you and with you I can just be myself and fully relaxed and at ease."

Perhaps this is the "oneness" it talks about in Genesis 2:24-25 where the ideal is to "become one flesh," and to be "naked" (or fully, transparently ourselves?) with each other and to feel "no shame." That's the kind of "comfortable" I'm talking about, and for us, it made love beautiful.

A Yucca Kind of Love

I want to say as strongly as I can that our love didn't just happen. It's not something we fell into. Our love was the product of a long, slow build. It was not just a by-product of lucky compatibility. In fact, we were not naturally all that compatible, as I'll share a little later.

Our love was beautiful, not because we were exceptionally gifted or because we did extraordinary things. Every day we practiced things that were very simple and yet surprisingly effective. We didn't discover some secret formula for success. There was no instant transformation. We didn't fall for each other and then live happily ever after. Instead, we practiced love. We "walked" in love. We "did" love, and that's how our love kept growing.

Writing about the growth of our love reminds me of the plant I bought Mary when we had been married for eighteen months. I wanted to do something to mark that mini-anniversary. I went to a plant nursery and said I wanted to buy a plant for my wife. The lady asked what kind of plant I wanted. I said I didn't know, but I hoped she could help me find the right one if I described what I wanted.

I said I wanted a plant that would grow very slowly and steadily. I wanted one that would grow all year long, not just in a certain season. I didn't care whether the plant had flowers, but I wanted the plant itself to always be green and attractive. I didn't want to have to do exotic stuff to it, like feed it special foods or stake it or prune it. I wanted one that would thrive on every-day care. I wanted a tough plant, one that didn't have to be babied because our firstborn, Nathan was already bumping his way around our house in one of those walkers that were popular back then.

I wanted an easy plant. Not fussy, and everything having to be perfect. I wanted something Mary could keep for years and years, a plant that would just keep on growing.

I told the lady I wanted a plant to symbolize the way love can grow, and never stop growing. That's why it had to grow slowly. I didn't want us to run out of house before the plant ran out of growth.

The lady at the nursery gave me a funny look, but thankfully got into the spirit of things. After some hesitation she said the only thing she could think of that would grow like that was a Yucca plant, not the low, spiny kind, but the kind that grows on a stem. Half an hour later I was proudly driving one home.

I arrived home and pulled the plant from behind my back, told Mary I had a surprise for her on our mini-anniversary, and I think Mary was a little disappointed at first. It didn't look as impressive as a dozen red roses. It was a little crooked and somewhat scrawny. But then I explained what I wanted the Yucca to symbolize. I told her why I wanted to give her not just any plant, but this one. I told her what I had told the plant lady.

Mary gave me a beautiful and teary kiss. Then she immediately took the plant to water it.

She nurtured our Yucca for a long time. She grew to love it. Fifteen years later it was taller than I am, a plant with wonderful texture and a beautiful healthy green canopy. It was the centerpiece of our indoor plants.

The Yucca turned out to be a true symbol of our love. I wish I could invent an adjective, one that is a combination of strong, unstoppable, secure, deep, comfortable, understanding and passionate. Love-as-it's-meant-to-be? Maybe that's the word I'm looking for. That was the love between Mary and me.

Mary's Yucca was only about elbow height, about 16 inches tall when I gave it to her. But as we gave it what it needed, it never stopped growing.

When love is nourished it never has to stop growing. When that happens, love too can be outstanding. That, my friends, is a beautiful thing. A thing worth writing about.

A Cancer Kind of Love

Our love-walk was tragically interrupted when cancer came into our lives.

It came suddenly and without warning. One day, we were comfortably in love; the next we were dealing with the fact that Mary had stage 4 Colon Cancer. It was a complete surprise. There was no warning whatsoever. We spent about two weeks in shock and virtual silence. For hours we sat together in our living room, holding on to each other. Sometimes we stood close, swaying together in slow dances for half an hour or more. Sometimes we just held each other's hand as we sat side by side.

We said very little, watching the moon over the frozen lake outside our window. Time slowed. We savored every moment we had together. We didn't want the moments to end. We didn't know what was ahead.

Not too long after that, something changed for me. All of my life to that point, I had lived in blissful ignorance about cancer. I had ignored it, and lived as though it would ignore me. Now ignorance wasn't so blissful, and suddenly I couldn't ignore cancer anymore. I no longer wanted to ignore it. I began to learn everything I could about cancer. I borrowed books and bought books, and read books on-line. I read early in the morning, after my devotions, and sometimes when I couldn't sleep at night. I read on weekends and on lunch breaks at work. I read testimonial books by cancer-survivors, and I read reports by researchers and doctors. I read studies, and journals of Oncology. I read thousands and thousands of pages, trying to answer a single question: "What can we do to help Mary fight cancer?"

I tried to read with discretion. There is much misinformation about cancer, and there are many people trying to profit from other people's misfortune. But I did read, and am still reading. I learned many surprising things about cancer. I learned many things I wish I had known, earlier.

Cancer is one of those things most people secretly fear, and don't want to talk about. It's almost as if we think by talking about it we are somehow inviting it into our lives, like we're jinxing ourselves.

Or perhaps we're more fatalistic than that. If someone is going to get cancer, they are going to get cancer, and there's nothing we can do about that, so no point talking about it!

For whatever reason, it doesn't make very good conversation in our circles. And it didn't make very much conversation in the circle of our family, even though there has been a significant history of cancer, especially on Mary's side. We didn't talk about it much, but I think we should have. After all my reading I have come to believe that for many, cancer can be preventable. I find myself wondering if Mary's cancer was possibly preventable. If only we had talked it up, and known the things we should have.

I usually spend a few minutes of my lunch hour scanning the news online. Just this week I caught a headline on Star.com that said, "Good news about cancer rates, what you can do to cut the risk." You know what I did with the article? I skimmed it first to see if I thought it was worth reading. Lots of stuff on cancer isn't. You don't really get a feel for that until you've read quite a bit.

When I saw the article was worth reading, I not only read it twice, I printed it so I could take it home and read it again, and add it to my growing binders of cancer information. The article is short, and to the point, talking about ways to prevent cancer, ways to ensure early detection of cancer, and ways to enhance treatment. It's a good article, with concise and accurate information that could have helped me if I had read it a few years ago.

But you know what would have happened if I had run across that article a few years ago? I might have started to read it, but probably not. Even if I did begin to read it, unless something in the story "hooked" me to make me want to keep reading, I would have quickly lost interest, and moved on to something more important to me, like the sports pages.

I guess what I'm saying is this. Some of the information I should have known has been there for decades. But I just wasn't interested in learning the information about cancer, even though it's not all that complicated. Back then, I didn't care enough to know. But that's not how it is now. That has changed. Now that Mary is gone, it's not for her sake anymore. It's for the rest of us. I don't want us needlessly to lose another Mary. It hurts way too much, doesn't it? I cried myself to sleep again the night I wrote those words. It's that kind of pain.

I want Mary's story to move the rest of us out of our complacency if at all possible. And I want her story to help us move from our collective unwillingness to think or talk much about cancer.

When Mary's cancer was discovered it changed our lives. It changed our walk in many ways. Some things were very difficult. On certain levels, life became much worse. But in other ways life became much better. We learned how to live, how to really live, with cancer. And it wasn't all bad. In many ways our lives became much richer.

Our love was already deep, but it became even deeper. We discovered things about each other that we never could have known. Parts of our faith and character grew in ways they never would have. We learned to pray like we had never prayed before. Worship became one of the most positive and precious things in our lives. It became a pillar of strength for us.

Our relationships with family members and our brothers and sisters in Christ were deepened. We were surrounded with more love than we ever knew existed. In many ways, the last year we had together was the very best year of our life, particularly the last five months, in spite of Mary's advancing cancer. The walk was sweeter than ever before.

We made some mistakes. We did some things right. We learned a lot about living. And we learned a lot about dying with dignity and grace and love and hope. I was intimately close when my best friend, my life-partner, my lover died. Mary didn't just die; she died *well*. No matter how emphatically I write that, it is an understatement, as I'll share later.

And now, in the months since my wife's death, I am learning a lot about the valley of grief, and how to keep on *living*, even there. I'm learning how to walk alone. I'm learning to live a life that is thankful for the past (even cancer?), rejoicing in the present (is that even possible?), and confident in the future.

REFLECTION

On Love

1. Think about Mary's "yucca" plant. On a scale of 1-10 (1=not very much, 10=completely), how well does that plant symbolize your love?

2. List at least three things you can do to ensure your love resembles that plant (always green and growing, the centrepiece of your life).

a.

b.

c.

3. How do you think having a symbol for your love could actually be helpful?

4. Mary and I were never hesitant to display our love in public. Just to be clear, I'm not talking about "making out" in public. I'm talking about things like politeness, holding doors, walking hand in hand, sitting close, kissing one another if we were meeting up somewhere—even if it was in public—and always speaking well of one another. Even though that seems to be out of vogue in our society today, was it wrong of us to be cross-cultural in demonstrating public affection? What positive effects might it have actually had on our relationship?

5. Why do you think so many couples seem to stop growing in their love?

On Cancer

1. Are you comfortable talking and thinking about cancer? If not, do you perhaps have kind of a "superstitious" attitude when it comes to talking about cancer? What might point to that?

2. Does having a superstitious attitude about cancer actually make sense? I'm going out on a limb here, and telling you I think it doesn't. Do you agree with me? Why/why not?

3. Does the thought of cancer make you afraid? Based on what I wrote in chapter one, why should fear actually not be given much place when it comes to cancer?

4. This question is meant to prime your thinking for a later discussion. If I asked you to name ten foods that fight cancer (and prevent it), could you name them? Do you actually consume them as a regular and conscious part of your diet?

How accurate would it be to say you even have a conscious diet, and that your health is the main criteria of that diet?

5. Have you allowed known carcinogens (like tobacco/asbestos/heavy metals/seared red meat) to be an ongoing part of your life? If so, what or who could help you break free from that?

2. The Power of Words

Big things were happening back then. It was spring of 1972. North America was in turmoil. Vietnam was on everyone's mind. Watergate was just beginning to break. Apollo 16 and the ongoing space-race were always in the news. The civil rights movement was getting a lot of press. Much of Canada was caught up in "Trudeau-mania," and the build up to hockey's Summit Series coming that fall.

But not too much of that was heavy on my mind. I was seventeen, soon to be eighteen, and preoccupied with more personal things. I had been playing at love for about two years. I had hurt my first girlfriend rather cruelly. I had "dumped" her without warning. That's what we called it when someone unilaterally called off the boyfriend-girlfriend thing. And a little later I got dumped myself. Big ouch! I mean huge ouch. It hurt me so badly I almost committed suicide. I literally came within inches of crashing the shop's work truck full speed into a huge tree. I was aiming straight for it, but at the last second, something or Someone pulled me back. But, that's another story. I mention it only so you'll know how it was for me in the spring of '72.

For me, love was something I was getting a bit more cautious about. Okay, a lot more cautious about, though I thought about it all the time, like about every three seconds. I often wondered if I'd ever experience real love. I was hungry for it, but at the same time afraid of it.

A Few Small Words

Then a small thing happened. A very small thing. A comment was made, a remark, just a few words from my younger brother, Ed. Three words to be exact. He was only fifteen, and had been dating a girl in his class, Wilma Molenaar. It's difficult to get around when you live out of town and want to date and you're only fifteen. So having my licence and a car, I got talked into being a chauffeur for a couple of their dates. Not something I'd recommend. It can be painfully quiet in the front seat when it's noisy in the back.

My brothers and I were downstairs in the rec room. We were a mostly-boy family, and ours really was more like a "wreck" room. Cement walls, lights covered with expanded metal, a net at either end, and four to six brothers sweating it out, going steel-toe to steel-toe with a hard puck and full contact body checking in our regular after-supper hockey game. We were catching our breath after a goal, and as brothers sometimes do, were talking about girls. And that's when Ed made this off-the-cuff remark about Wilma's older sister, Mary.

Mary was the same age as me, but in the class behind mine. She was very good looking, and recently unattached.

Ed began with a question, designed I'm sure to get my full attention. "Hey, Bert, do you know who kinda likes you?" I leaned on my stick; a guy has to keep his cool, but on the inside I was all ears. A pause for effect, then came three little words.

"Mary likes you!"

Small Words, Big Impact

That's all. The words were a remark, but spoken with a hint of pronouncement. I should have written them like this: "*MARY LIKES YOU!*", because that's how the words played in my mind.

Three little words. But words can grow on you. They did for me. And it was those three little words that got Mary and I walking. The words didn't take too long to blossom into an idea about Mary. It was a new idea for me. I had known Mary as a casual friend for about three years already. In fact, she was one of the girls we Michel boys would often give a ride home after school. My Dad had purchased a Volkswagen Beetle (the original Beetle, a gutless wonder), so we could drive instead of taking the bus, and get home in time to do a solid hour's work in the welding shop before supper. One of our teen pleasures was to stuff as many girls in the car with us as we could, and give them a ride to their homes along our way. Sometimes there would be ten or twelve people crammed in there, usually more than one girl for every guy. There were no seatbelt laws back then, so we really did cram them in. We thought it was mighty nice of us to give those girls a ride home. Of course, it never crossed our minds to offer guys a ride.

So I knew Mary that way, and found her to be a pleasant person. But I had never even thought of her in a romantic way. She had been going steady with a guy in my class for quite a while, and one of the understandings we had among the guys was that you didn't mess with someone else's girl. So I never even thought of romance when it came to Mary. But they were no longer a couple.

Those three words wouldn't have been spoken a few months before. But now they had, and now definite thoughts of romance began to form in my mind.

Maybe this was something of an opportunity? Maybe I could get back into the love game in a low-risk way? I mean, it is way less risky asking someone out if you have inside information that they actually like you! And besides, Ed wanted to go out with Wilma, so there would be even less risk if I made it sound less like I was asking her out on a real date.

The idea taking shape, I boldly threw caution to the wind and called her. "Hey Mary, its Bert. I was talking to Ed and he wants to take Wilma to (I forget the event, I think it was an extracurricular school thing). So I'm giving them a ride. Do you want to tag along?"

Mary rather quickly agreed. After a few of those semi-dates, and finding her to be very pleasant company indeed, I asked her out for our first real date. Our school hockey team was part of a church league that held a hockey banquet every year. It was a formal banquet with awards ceremonies. Almost all the players would take a date. So I asked Mary to go with me (no one else tagging along), and got an immediate yes.

She and her mom made a dress, a beautiful full-length, with a delicate floral print, kind of creamy yellowish-pink. I can close my eyes, and still see her wearing it. She gave me a swatch of the material a week ahead of time, and I bought her a corsage to match. I recall pinning it on her dress, at the start of our evening, with a bit of a tremble in my hands. I felt like I was touching something very beautiful.

I remember almost nothing about the banquet, other than it being in Peterborough. But I remember the ride home. We "parked" for a while in an isolated spot, and that was our first kiss. It was our first kiss in my first car, a 1963 Volvo 544 fast-back, B-18 engine, burnt-brown in color.

More Small Words

Fast forward almost thirty-nine years. It is January, 2011. We've raised four children (Nathan, Adam, Sara and Aimee). Mary and I are empty nesters now, and loving every minute of it. Our love is a grown-up love now. Just the summer before, we celebrated 35 years of marriage with our first big vacation, an Alaskan cruise. We feel so fortunate to be married to one another.

Again I hear a few little words that are the start of something bigger. These words are also spoken in a "wreck" room. It's the recovery room of the Health Centre, in Mooseport, Ontario. I've slipped back to work while Mary undergoes a routine colonoscopy. It's been five years since the last one, and while it's not pleasant, with her nursing background, and with cancer in her family, Mary knows it is one of those things she just has to do. Mary is so good at stuff like that, never complaining or postponing, just doing what needs to be done.

I get a little work finished, and they call me to say I can pick her up now. In ten minutes, I'm back in Mooseport and a little surprised to find myself waiting for Mary. Why would they call me to come for her, then make me wait? I'm not upset, just a little curious. A nurse comes through the endoscopy unit door and calls my name. "Bert, you can come in to see Mary now."

"See her?" I said to myself. "I thought I was here to pick her up?"

I follow the nurse through the doors and around the corner and there is Mary. She is sitting on a low stool, looking very small. Her back is to the wall. The stool is so low that her knees are prominent as I come toward her. She is looking a little confused, still influenced by the anaesthetic.

She is leaning forward, hunched over her knees, arms partly wrapped around them. It looks like she is cold. I walk toward her, and our eyes meet. I smile at her, but the smile I get in return is a little crooked. She's dazed.

Our surgeon is sitting on a stool next to her, one hand on her knee. He isn't smiling. He acknowledges me, then turns to Mary, and says, "So Mary, about your cancer..."

Time slows. The words hang in the air. Something seems wrong with the words. They shouldn't be said so bluntly and factually should they? They couldn't be so factual could they? But there isn't an "if" or a "maybe" or even a hint of a question. The words are presented as facts. The doctor is very pointed. Mary has a tumor, a large tumor. It is positively cancerous. It is almost blocking Mary's bowels. It has to come out soon. Surgery has already been booked for two weeks from today. Any questions?

None that we can think of. And then the doctor leaves the room, and I help Mary up and give her a gentle, extended hug. One of the nurses comes over. It's Helena, a long-time friend and sister in Christ. She's the operating room nurse today. She's been crying. She gives Mary a long hug too.

Oh God, Help Me Say the Right Thing

We head to the car. It is winter. I help Mary in then close the passenger door. Open my door, sit down and shut the door. Start the engine. Let it warm up for a while. We sit in silence, each thinking our own thoughts. Mine are slow and

21

jumbled. Everything is slow. I'm thinking about the doctor's words and how they've changed everything. I'm thinking about Mary and what it might be like to hear those words. There are things I want to say to her. I feel so unprepared, but I have a strong feeling that I should say something. The silence lingers. I'm letting the car warm up way longer than I usually do. I sense that this is one of those times when what I say really matters. I want to get it right. I'm aware that I could say the wrong thing. I don't want this to be one of those times. I pray for words.

It would have been far easier to just put the car in gear and drive. To wait for a better time to say something if I must. To wait until I get it right. But love won't let me wait.

"Mary," (I hold her hand and wait for full eye contact) "there's something I want to say to you. I'm not sure how to put it exactly, but something inside me is telling me I need to say this to you. So here goes.

"Mary, I love you no matter what happens, and I'll walk with you through everything that is ahead of us. It's not just you that has cancer, it's us. With all that I am and all that I have I will be there for you. I'll be there for every doctor's appointment and every treatment. I'll never leave you to face this alone. This doesn't make me love you less. It makes me love you more."

My eyes hold hers. Tears are streaming down her face, mine too. She thanks me and says she loves me too. We're still holding hands and share a long, tearful kiss. It's a lingering kiss. I keep her hand in mine as we slowly drive home. I can tell she doesn't want me to let go, and I don't want to either.

Why the Words were Right

I think back to those moments and am so glad I told Mary what I did. Somehow I was given to say to her exactly what she needed to hear. You see, most women have a secret fear about their husbands, even in a good marriage. They know they love their husbands, but secretly fear he doesn't really love them to the same degree. Most women never get past needing reassurance on that front. Does he really love me like I love him, and is he really loyal to me?

This doubt is compounded by the fact that women have eyes which actually work (usually better than a man's!). And those eyes see what tends to happen when a woman gets sick. Sickness calls for nurture, and nurture is not a big part of most men's skill-set is it? It's not all that unusual for men to let their women down, if not physically – by being absent – then at least emotionally.

In fact, Mary and I were both familiar with Dr. Emerson Eggerichs' book, *Love and Respect*. We had taught it together to a number of couples in pre-marital counselling. In the book, the author wants to make a point about this whole love and loyalty question. He quotes a distinguished oncologist (cancer doctor) who had long experience in dealing with dying people as saying, "Almost all women stand by their men. Very few men stand by their women." (p. 170)

Walking through fourteen rounds of chemotherapy would later confirm that statement. We saw literally hundreds of patients getting treatment. Almost without fail, when we saw a man getting chemotherapy, his wife was there caring for him, walking him through the hardship. Not so the other way around. In almost every case, when a woman was there getting treatment she was helped and accompanied by a daughter or a sister or a friend. I sometimes felt conspicuous. Was it because their men had to work? That might be what they told themselves. I think it was because men tend not to stand by their women when they are in circumstances that involve her health. It's doubly so for something like cancer, where everything is out of one's control, and makes a man feel helpless. Cancer is something you can't fix. And if a man can't fix something, he tends to run.

What Women Fear

As I said before, women have eyes that work. They are not blind to the fact that men often run when their wives face a serious disease. So for Mary, that was no doubt one of her intuitive fears as she sat there in our car. Was she perhaps thinking about the disfigurement that can come from cancer? "What if cancer makes me ugly?" Mary was a nurse. She had seen what advanced cancer can do to a person's appearance. "I'm not 29 anymore, and now I have cancer? Will he still find me attractive? Will he still love me like he did? Will this change his love for me?" [2]

For whatever reason, I felt I had to give her a two-fold message: "I will be there for you," and "this makes me love you more." My only regret looking back is that I could have said those things to her more often in the following year and a half. I said them at the beginning, and I repeated them to her more than once, but I probably should have done it more. Would finding a way to say them every day have been too much? Overkill, maybe. But every week would probably have been about right.

Saying Good Words

By the time we heard the word cancer, Mary and I knew how to speak good words to each other. We knew about the power of words, and that it isn't enough to just say nothing when you are not sure what to say. We knew that words have power

---

[2] I found out recently that Mary confided those very thoughts to our daughter. I'm so thankful God led me to answer those exact questions, even though I habitually missed a lot of things with Mary. It's a man thing to miss sometimes, but I think it was a God thing to not miss it this time.

between people. They often have disproportionate power. When talking about words - the product of our tongues - in the Bible, James uses the analogy of a rudder and a ship. Big ship, small rudder, but the small thing is what steers the much bigger (James 3:4). The tongue too is little, but it can strongly affect the direction of our lives. Just a few words can make things better, but they can also make things much worse.

We discovered this early in our relationship. I remember getting angry with Mary one time. We had been dating for a year or two. By now, we were officially a "couple". We were at my parents' house on a Sunday afternoon. Mary accidentally did something that really hurt me, stomping on my bare foot with one of these wooden sandals she used to wear back then. I never liked those sandals in the first place. I had not yet learned to control my temper, and I yelled at her to just get out of here and leave me alone! She looked at me a little confused, like, where and how was she supposed to go? We were at my place and she didn't have a car.

So I yelled at her again, "Yeah, just get out of here! Take my car, get out of here, and don't bother coming back!"

Mary's eyes were always the most expressive thing about her. She gave me this look, a wounded look. Then she squared her shoulders, said nothing, got into my Pontiac (my second car, a 1954 Pontiac Chieftan, two-door, all original, exactly our age, seats-like-a-couch, flat-head six cylinder, three on the tree, gutless, but I kind of liked that car too), and drove off. My foot stopped hurting about the same time my tail lights were disappearing up Simcoe Street and over Purple Hill.

It dawned on me that this was not a very good situation, that my words had caused a lot of damage, and that I really didn't want her to go and not come back. So I waited half an hour, enough time to make sure she got home (there were no cell phones back then so what else could I do?), phoned her place, asked for Mary, and apologized for my words. I told her I was sorry, and that I didn't want her to leave and not come back. I asked her to please still go out with me.

That wounded look in her eyes was bothering me a lot, so I added a promise. "Mary, I'll never yell at you again, ever!" She took the yelling thing very seriously. She said she'd still go out with me, but that if I ever yelled at her again, that would be it, she'd end our relationship. She'd had time to think about that on the drive home, and I knew she meant it. So I never yelled at her again.

I was telling our second son, Adam about this the other day and he said he remembered one time when I yelled at her. It was after about ten years of marriage, when we had just moved from our original log home into a semi-detached home in Mooseport. Mary had gone shopping for some stuff for the new house, I think it was curtains, but when she came back, she said she had also seen some furniture on sale at Sears, and she had bought a couch and chairs for our living room.

Adam says he remembers me yelling, "You did WHAT?" I don't remember yelling. I do remember being surprised. But if I yelled at her it couldn't have been too bad because I don't remember any wounded eyes. I'd have remembered those, and besides, we kept the furniture.

You see, by then we had learned the power of words for good or evil in a relationship. And we lived by some very simple rules. We wanted our home to be a place where uplifting things were said. Both of us had grown up where the response to trouble was sometimes anger and frustration rather than calm discussion and conversation. When that happened, we felt yelled at, rather than listened to. Neither of us wanted our home to be a place where there was yelling.

Our Word Rules

So we made some simple rules about words in our home.

1. As parents, we would never fight or even disagree about anything in front of our kids. If we disagreed, we would talk about it in private, and always present a united front to our children. We had been practicing that for a long time before they became teens. Smart move I think! Some modern relationship experts would disagree with me. They

would say we were robbing our kids of a positive role model. We should have shown then how to disagree, and work out the disagreement in an adult fashion, even a loud one. I think they are wrong. Kids wouldn't even notice any good in that role model. They'd be too busy feeling the insecurity. Kids need security and love more than a fighting role model as I see it. For whatever it's worth, it was our rule, and it was good for us.

2. As a couple, we would talk things out instead of being angry with each other. If we happened to become angry, we would resolve the anger that very day. We took seriously what it says in Ephesians 4:26 – "In your anger, do not sin. Do not let the sun go down when you are still angry." For us, the promise to each other was that we would never go to sleep while still angry with each other. A few times, it meant we didn't go to sleep until very late. Mary could be very stubborn! (Okay... so could I.) But we never let the day end in anger or disagreement. It always had to end in love. Again, I've read modern experts who disagree. They say that keeping something going until late at night just leads to a deepening of the fight. They advocate calling a "truce" until morning, then resolving it when you have better energy to do it. I'd argue that they are wrong. If Mary and I had tried that, I know we would *not* have been better equipped in the morning. I'd have had a restless sleep. And knowing Mary, she wouldn't have slept at all.

3. We would not yell at our kids. Ever. We'd talk to them in an adult tone, and we'd be a safety net for each other in that regard. If Mary started to raise her voice, I'd step in and say, "Hon, can I handle this?" And she'd do the same for me. And it would be a "signal" between us, that our voice was beginning to be raised. We had a certain "look" we would give each other, a thing we would do with our eyebrows. The firm agreement between us was that no matter what the issue, if that "signal" came out, we would immediately back off. Sometimes I did it for her; other times she did it for me. I'm not saying we *never* yelled at our kids. I'm sure they'd tell you there were times. But I'm also sure they'd tell you that yelling was a rare exception because we had made this a rule between us.

4. We decided that the words "I love you" would be spoken every day between the two of us, and from us to our children. It became the first thing Mary heard every morning. I would tiptoe into our room before going to work, kiss her good-bye, and say, "I love you." She would kiss me back, and say "I love you too," then doze for a while before she got up. She always woke to a kiss and "I love you." How good is that?

When I got home from work, or when she got home from a shift, it would be a kiss and always the same words. And at night, the last thing before sleeping was always, "I love you," and "I love you too!" Sometimes she would say it first, sometimes I would. But it was always what we said instead of

"Good night!" If we did say "Good night," the words "I love you" were still to come.

Simple words, "I love you". We said them to each other up to ten times a day. But oh how powerful those three little words are if you want your love to grow.

Power in Words

Words have more power than we think. I'm reminded that the Lord God *spoke* things into being at creation, and *calls* (another form of speaking) us into becoming a new creation. It shouldn't surprise us that as His image-bearers our words would have creative power in our relationships. I'm pretty sure that with Mary and me, our "speaking" love had a lot to do with the fact that we continued to grow in love.

We took the speaking thing further than that too. In the Dutch-Canadian subculture of our upbringing, and growing up in the turbulent times of the sixties and seventies, sarcasm and put-downs were a big part of daily speech. Trash-talking was common even among friends and between couples. As young people, and as a young couple, our talk, mostly mine, was rough. We were already saying "I love you," to each other, but early on, we also trashed each other in our speech. Trashing each other was even part of our flirting.

Mostly to Mary's credit, it didn't stay that way. She didn't like demeaning talk of any kind. She was very sensitive to it, and to the fact that people pretended to be okay with it. She didn't push that on me; simply let me know how she felt about it. So a quiet transformation came over us. The change was mostly on my part. She was way ahead of me here. The absence of trash talk started early, and became an established pattern between us. After the first two years of our relationship it wasn't who we were anymore.

Low-Powered Words

We had been married for about seventeen years and were living near Sault Ste. Marie, Ontario. I had always played hockey, and was becoming friends with our new next-door neighbor, Sam. Sam played hockey in the Industrial League in the Sault, and found out that I played. He invited me to come to their first practice and consider joining the team. I went, and really enjoyed the hockey. It was at a pretty challenging level. They thought I was a good enough D-man to join the team, so I played that year. Like I said, I enjoyed the hockey. But I only played about half the season before I quit the team even though I had prepaid.

It wasn't that it was a beer league, even though I'm not a fan of the way beer can make people stupid. It was the way they talked that got to me, took all the fun out of the game for me.

Not the fact that they swore a lot. I had lived in the welding and trucking worlds long enough not to be put off by that. It was the way they trash-talked their wives. Most of the guys were about my age, most were married. The ones that were not had girlfriends. The way they talked about women made me sick. I know some of it was just guy-talk, but I never heard one positive comment about their significant others. It was all put-downs and crude jokes and comments that made her out to be a nag at best. It was so persistent in that dressing room that it just wasn't fun for me to be there. I quietly quit. I actually gave up hockey!

I tell you that to highlight the verbal change that was central to our relationship by then. The dressing room talk was different only in degrees from the way I used to talk myself. But for years our talk had been totally different. Mary had never belittled me, even in jest. By then, I never talked down to her or about her, whether she was there, or if she was absent. I never told "wife" jokes, even if there is the odd one that's almost irresistibly funny. She was never in my jokes. Instead, I talked well of her, or said nothing at all.

The Long-Term Effect

Looking back, I noticed something. Mary was actually quite shy. She didn't like being the center of attention (except on her wedding day, but then she had a white dress to hide behind).

When we first got married, she was hesitant about her opinions, even with me. She was shy of being creative. She had definite tastes in things like decorating, but she always toned it down, "settling" for it even if she didn't really "love it". For years when we painted the house she always wanted me to choose the colors. Always.

I think looking back, she was afraid to be put down. I'm sure it was a by-product of her grade school days. She had failed grade three, and that inevitably leads to a put-down feeling. It was made worse by the fact that one of her teachers back then, one of her authority figures, told her flat-out one day, "Mary Molenaar, you are just stupid. You'll never amount to much of anything!" She was young and tender, and things like that go deep. Those bullying words stayed with her a long time.

But the longer we were married, the more she was shaped by better words. She was growing bolder with her opinions, especially with me. It wasn't until the middle years of our marriage that she actually began to pray out loud. She did it with me first, and then with other people too. Before that, she had always been too shy for that. She had always told me, "You pray for us." About the same time that she began praying out loud, she also began to experiment more with colors and flowers and even with some of the clothing she wore and her hairstyle. It made me love her even more as I was discovering more and more about her strengths.

I don't think it was an accident that Mary's view of herself began to change after the negative speech patterns in our relationship were gone. I'm not saying we'd "arrived" or anything like that. I'm just saying we'd moved a long way from where we started, and it was good. In the last fifteen years of our marriage, when we were painting, she always chose the colors. Always! Even when I wasn't sure about her choice, I'd go with it, and inevitably it would turn out to be beautiful.

I've been thinking here about words and their power, what they can begin and what they can build. They do have surprising power don't they? And I'm so thankful that by the time Mary was diagnosed with cancer our love was rich in words. I cannot imagine how much more difficult the cancer journey would have been if it were not for the power of words.

REFLECTION

1. I invite you, even urge you to think about the way words are used in your home and in your significant relationship. Do they help your partner to grow? Do they consistently build up the other person?

2. If the day comes for you to hear a shocking diagnosis, how can you ensure that your established speech patterns be such that you will be

able to "nail it," and speak true life-words to your spouse?

3. When I use the term "life-words" what do you think I mean? How do the following two verses add to your understanding of what life-words are?

Colossians 4:6

"Let your conversation always be full of grace, seasoned with salt."

Ephesians 4:29-30

"Do not let any unwholesome talk come out of your mouths, but only what is helpful for building others up according to their needs, that it may benefit those who listen. And do not grieve the Holy Spirit of God."

4. Review the rules of speech Mary and I practiced. Rank them in order of their importance to you.

1-

2-

3-

4-

5. Which of the following do you think most accurately describes the effect of words, and why?

a) The quality of your relationship is directly proportional to the quality of the words between you.

b) The quality of your relationship governs the quality of the words between you.

c) The quality of the words between you has some effect on the quality of your relationship.

d) The quality of the words between you has very little effect on the quality of your relationship.

6. When I told Mary those two things right after her diagnosis, should I have added anything? How could I have said things better?

7. Mary's teacher had a profoundly negative impact on her. Have you experienced that kind of negative word-impact in your life? How can the negative power of that be broken for you?

3. When You Don't Feel Ready

Sometimes things happen to you even if you don't feel like you are ready for them. You only realize you were ready in hindsight. It was like that for me when it came to loving Mary.

We had been going on dates for a few months. And I liked her. She was really nice. I even kissed her because she was so nice. There was certainly an attraction. But I didn't think what I was feeling for her was love. I was actually still a bit afraid of love. Remember, I'd hurt and been hurt just a few months before that. So had she. It was fun playing the game of romance with her. It sure beat walking alone. But I wasn't so sure about love. My uncertainty almost ended our relationship.

We had been dating since spring of 1972. Two months later my parents sent me to a Christian Youth Conference in Bolton, Ontario for a weekend. The conference was aimed at straightening out some of my youthful rebellion. There was quite a bit of tension in the Michel home back then because a lot of us were teens. The conference featured a high-powered speaker. I remember he was pretty good, very forceful, though I don't recall a thing he said.

I do remember hanging out at that conference with a girl from my class, Angela, whom I had known for four years and who happened to have been sent by her parents to the conference also. Angela and I were good friends. Not a romantic thing, but good friends. Ours was a unique high-school class, where a lot of us, male and female, just cared about each other as people. So Angela and I hung around and talked in the spare times during that weekend conference.

We talked quite a bit about God. We were both struggling with the hypocrisy we saw in our family and church. It actually made us angry. To our young eyes, many of the people who had the right "look" on Sunday could sure beat up on you on Monday. They could be downright mean. We talked back and forth about God, and whether He was real, or if it was all just words. We wondered about whether He was worth following, and if He was real, how could He allow hypocritical things to just go on and on?

The last night of the conference we had skipped out on the evening session, and were hanging around outside, evading the armed guards (okay, they weren't armed, but supervisors made sure we were in all the sessions). We somehow outmaneuvered them, and ended up hiding and talking in her car.

It was one of those rare nights with an incredibly full moon and brilliant starlight. We were far enough outside the city limits to be treated to a dazzling night sky. I was in awe. We were so small, and the sky was so grand. It was truly a Psalm 19:1 experience, "The heavens declare the glory of God; the skies proclaim the work of his hands." They sure were declaring that night! I remember Angela asking if we shouldn't really believe in God when we saw stuff like the sky above us. I thought maybe I agreed, and she said maybe we should pray to Him, or something. So I prayed the first honest prayer I'd prayed in a long time. I didn't want to pray anything even remotely hypocritical, since we'd been talking a lot about that. So I uttered words like, "God, I'm not even really sure if you're there or not. But what I see around me and above me leads me to believe you probably are. If you really are there, and you're listening to me, help me be sure about it. Show Yourself to me. That's it I guess." I didn't even want to say "Amen," because it sounded too religious. Angela prayed too. And then it was quiet for quite a while.

Leading Mary On?

Then Angela asked me about Mary, and how our relationship was going. Angela and I had the kind of platonic friendship where we could talk about stuff like that. I confided that I wasn't too sure about love, wasn't too sure if I was ready for love, and that Mary seemed to be more sure of it than I was. So Angela asked me if I thought that was being fair to Mary. She was Mary's friend too, and almost seemed to be defending Mary. We talked about that for quite a while, and I decided maybe it really wasn't fair to Mary, and that the right thing to do would probably be to not date her anymore, to not be leading her on.

It was one thing to talk about it at some distance from Mary. It was quite another to try to verbalize it to her on our next date. We had already planned one for the weekend after the conference. I remember struggling quite a bit with this whole thing as the evening approached. *How do I talk about this without hurting Mary? I don't want to hurt her. She is a beautiful person. I really do like her.*

10 Seconds of Mercy

So we go out, and when the date is over, we are sitting in my car, the Volvo again, in the Molenaar family driveway. I tell her there's something I really need to talk to her about. I give her the whole speech I've been rehearsing in my mind. About how it isn't her, but it's me. And that I really like her and think she is a great person, and how I don't want to hurt her, but I just don't think I am actually ready for love.

I even use the classic line, "Can we just be good friends?" I am kind of embarrassed, fumbling with my words, sort of looking down as I am telling her all this.

She doesn't say anything, not a word or question, just sits there and listens. Our relationship is about ten seconds away from being over. I remember those ten seconds like they happened yesterday. Upon reflection, I think it was a God-moment, one of those times when He intervenes and turns things in a completely different direction than you had planned. Sometimes he does it so fast, you don't even know it's happening. I'll never be anything but grateful for those ten seconds of mercy, though they were very confusing for Mary.

I had been stumbling along for a while, and I had kind of run out of words. So I lifted my head, and looked at her. Here's where the ten seconds start. I'm not sure what I was expecting, or what made me lift my head. But I look at her, and was immediately captured by her eyes. They were riveting. She was looking straight at me. I saw a depth there that I had never seen before. This wasn't just some girl-toy, someone to play at romance with. This was a woman, a beautiful woman. In those deep blue eyes was a looked that mixed love and pain. It took my breath away.

And suddenly an intense feeling welled up inside me, seeming to come from nowhere. After all I had just said to her, I felt this sudden and overwhelming love for her. It was powerful. It was real. It was unlike anything I had felt for her before. It was unlike anything I had felt for any girl before.

So acting on impulse, I did what a guy has to do. Without a word, I leaned in and gave her a strong, firm, long, emphatic, searching kiss, right on the lips. Not a goodbye kiss. Not a quick peck, but the best lover's kiss I could muster in the intensity of the moment.

How confusing for Mary! The poor, dear young woman. It was suddenly too much for her!

Breaking off the kiss, she jerked back from me, burst into tears, threw open the car door, and ran into her house, and for all I knew, out of my life forever.

I found out later that her mother was in the kitchen when Mary came sobbing through the door. She took one look at Mary, put her hands on her hips (I'm glad I didn't follow Mary to the house, because Mary's mom could be a formidable matriarch when she stood like that) and said, "And JUST WHAT did HE DO to you?" It took a long, long time for Mary's mom to warm up to me after that, though she has loved me like a son for many years now.

Undoing the Mess

I drove off slowly. I was trying to process what had just happened, especially the strong feeling that had come over me. Without putting words to it, something in me recognized it as love. But had I ever messed things up! How on earth would I be able to undo what I had just done? It was a long ride home.

There were a few restless days and nights while I tried to get up the courage to talk to Mary again. But I finally did, and phoned to see if I could please come and talk to her. So I came to her place, and she met me outside, and we talked. She was the cautious one now. She stood a little distance from me, her arms kind of folded in front of her as we talked. I remember some of her little sisters looking out from the window at us. This was high drama for them.

Mary asked me what I really wanted. I told her what had come over me that night, apologized for confusing her, said I thought I probably had got it wrong, that I was ready for love after all, and could she please give me another chance? Maybe we could back off, and start all over again? She wanted to know if I was sure. I said I thought I was. So we did start over again, a little more carefully, and a little more slowly. No promises that day, but a mutual agreement that we'd just give it a try.

And from that day on we were together. There was never a doubt after that. We were us. There was a new balance. Love wasn't such a one-way street anymore. Both of us were beginning to love each other. It wasn't text-book, and I probably wouldn't recommend that kind of dramatic stuff as a tactic for any relationship. You might not get your ten seconds of mercy. But that's how it happened between Mary and me.

Wedding Day Jitters

I wasn't sure I was ready at the beginning of our love. I was like that on our wedding day too. The morning of our wedding, I got cold feet. It was the first time since becoming an official couple that I had my doubts. I knew Mary loved me, and that I loved her, but the idea of "lifetime" was suddenly hitting me hard. I wasn't sure I was ready for that. We were only twenty years old. People change. What if she turned into someone I didn't like? What if she was a nag in ten years? What if she didn't look good to me anymore?

I remember considering it while I was getting dressed in my room, alone. As I was putting on my suit, I was thinking I didn't really want to go through with this today. Maybe we could just keep dating for a lot longer. I just didn't feel ready for marriage.

But as I thought about maybe not showing up, I also thought of all the work Mary had been doing to prepare for our wedding, and how she had loved every minute of it, even every hassle. With her mom's help she had made her own dress, and the bridesmaids' dresses. She had booked the hall, and arranged flowers and the meal, and the guest list, and all the stuff that had to be done. She had even purchased our bedroom suite and kitchen appliances. She had invested everything she had. I knew she had been looking forward to it. It was her dream day. So I knew it would just kill her spirit if I didn't show up. It would be the worst thing I could do to her.

So I thought better of everything I had been thinking. I went ahead with marriage even though I didn't feel ready for it at all. Apparently I wasn't the only one who wasn't sure how ready I was for marriage. Three times, Mary's dad turned to her on the way to the church and asked her, "Mary, are you sure about this? Because if you're not, I can turn the car around right now and you don't have to go ahead with it. You can say no right now, but if you say yes, then that's it. Then you don't come back to Mom and me." I think he was hoping Mary would say no.

I didn't find that out until years later. Mary never told me. She was wise that way. I do remember some of my uncles standing around that day, having a smoke after the ceremony, and I could read the doubt in their eyes as they looked at us. "Kids! They're just kids! They're not ready for marriage!"

As it turned out, I was very wrong and so was Dad and so were my uncles. I was ready for marriage, more than I ever knew.

Surprisingly Ready for Cancer

a) Physical Fitness

Sometimes you don't feel like you're ready for something but you are. It was like that with love and it was like that with marriage.

And it was like that with cancer too. Looking back, God did a number of things to make us ready. I say that because I don't think there were any accidents.

We were both in a good place physically. Oh sure, we could have lost a few pounds. But we hadn't let ourselves fall apart. In fact, one of the highlights of our recent Alaskan cruise was a hike down Mount Roberts, in Juneau. We took the tramway up, and were hiking the trails about 3,000 feet above the town. As we did, we noticed a sign saying, "Trail to Town 2 ½ miles," near the top of the mountain. It was a great day, so we decided to hike down. The trail was winding, very steep, and slippery because it had rained the night before. But there were enough trees to ensure it was not too dangerous. As we scrambled down through coastal rainforest, we saw two bald eagles and incredible vegetation. I had good hiking boots on, but Mary just had her runners. Frequently I had to go down one step, give Mary a foothold, then go down another. It took us over three hours of lung-stretching hard work. But we had no trouble doing stuff like that physically. We were not in perfect shape, but we were aerobically fit. We ate a reasonably balanced diet, and we did lots of active things like cleaning, home renovations, shovelling the driveway and gardening. We lived in a split-level home, so we involuntarily did a lot of stairs. Mary always went on a walk of her own in the morning, and most evenings we would walk together on the Crown Land near our home. In the winter, we often used the treadmill.

Cancer treatments can take such a toll on you that if you are not in a good place physically, you can go downhill very fast. Mary was thankfully strong – as strong as she had ever been. We were prepared that way.

b) Emotional and Spiritual Health

We found something to laugh about almost every day. Really, we laughed a lot. It wasn't too hard with our grandsons, Noah and Joel, living next door. Neither one of us was "down" about life. Both of us were emotionally balanced.

Cancer introduces many pressures, decisions, tensions, questions, uncertainties, frustrations, waiting and a sense that you are losing control of your life. If you are not in good emotional health when cancer strikes, you really will need the anti-depressants your doctor wants to prescribe. We were both in a positive place that way. So although we were offered them many times, we would never need an anxiety pill or even a sleeping pill. It's just where we were at.

We were also in a good place spiritually. We were in a good church where worship was rich and preaching was authentic. We were both systematically and regularly enjoying our own devotional times. Both of us had been keeping a spiritual journal for a few years. In them we kept track of the thoughts God gave us each day, and the scriptures that particularly spoke to us. We recorded prayer requests and answers. We were learning to pray much more boldly and specifically than we had before.

I look back at my own journals from those days and see instances of very specific prayers being answered. Work was extremely slow at the time, and I was praying for exact numbers of trailers to sell to get us through the hard times. Consistently, God was answering those prayers, and going beyond them. I was re-learning the gift of specific prayer.

There are two rounds of those "trailer" prayers. And then, suddenly, in the middle of the second round, my journal entries are no longer focused on trailers. It's not that I no longer prayed about those practical needs, but they are not the focus anymore. Mostly my entries were about a new and a bigger need. I was now writing prayers about Mary's cancer.

God was getting both of us ready by putting us in that place of rediscovering the power of trusting, specific prayer. Prayer became our immediate response to cancer. We had never even thought about being ready for cancer. But in the area of prayer, God had us ready.

We prayed together every day. It's how we closed our day, lying side by side in our bed, holding hands, and praying aloud. First we gave thanks for the day, and the things God had brought our way. Then we prayed about whatever "issue" was on our minds.

Finally we took turns praying for every one of our children and grandchildren by name. It was our habit every day, a very intentional practice. Praying about cancer just became an extension of the praying-together that was already there. Praying together was one of the gifts by which God had us ready to face cancer.

The Power of Community

We were also part of a small group ministry at our church. The group was one of the better ones we have been part of over the years. Our prayers were real, and we seldom let stuff stay at a surface level. We didn't just say the things we were "supposed" to say. We asked the hard questions that sometimes need to be asked. We were honest about it when we knew we missed the mark. We were learning to love each other as brothers and sisters in Christ, and to challenge one another in our faith. It was an encouraging group to be part of.

That group too, I believe was part of God's preparation. We had only joined it about a year earlier. We had been there long enough to really feel like we were a part of it. They became a huge emotional and spiritual lifeline during the entire cancer journey. Those wonderful people were really there for us, from the moment we found out about the cancer to the last day of Mary's life.

The very first meeting we had with them after discovering the cancer, they immediately ditched the agenda and we spent an extended time praying for Mary. It's all we did for an hour and a half. The whole group gathered around her, each person laying a hand on Mary as they interceded for her. It was incredibly moving.

When we were finished, all of us had tears in our eyes, and Mary gave each person in the group a long thank-you hug. The support of that group was with us through the entire cancer journey. The last few meetings we had were at our home. Even though we lived the furthest away from everyone, it's what the group wanted. They brought food, did all the work, and cleaned up. They did it just to make sure Mary could still be part of our circle. More than one of our meetings were devoted entirely to praying for Mary and me as the cancer journey got tougher. That precious group of God's people were the heart and hands of Christ to us.

God had us ready for this journey. We didn't know we were ready until well along the way. But we were. I never once saw Mary fall apart, or scream at God (or even life). I never saw her ask, "Why me?", or get depressed or even quit the fight when it got really tough. No one would have faulted her if she had reacted in some of those ways. But they never seemed to cross her mind. Instead, she remained calm and thankful and it was always a pleasure to be with her. People would come to give her comfort and strength, and instead find themselves comforted and strengthened. I'm still awed by it.

Reading Her Journals

As I read back through Mary's journals, which are a treasure to me, I keep seeing those things. There are words of faith and trust and love. It's consistent. For example, Saturday, February 4, 2012, she wrote, "Today I am weak. I need extra strength. So help me to walk this day as You have planned for me Lord. Then I will truly be strong in you."

The next day, Sunday, she wrote, "I am glad you are my leader, Lord, the one I can count on through thick and thin. So help me today to worship as you deserve. I love you Lord."

On Valentine's Day Mary was thinking about love. "Today people think about love. So I want to thank you dear Heavenly Father for your love to me. For Bert and his unconditional love, my kids and family who have blessed me this past year with abundant support and care. To God be the glory, great things He has done."

Skip ahead to the month of May, when she was beginning to fail rapidly; the tone doesn't change at all. Even on Tuesday, May 8, 2012. It was just a few weeks before she died, and the doctors had ordered another C.T. scan to discern if her liver was failing. Mary hated the scans. Getting the I.V. started was such a trial and hurt her so much. Her veins had always been tiny, but they were getting harder and harder to find. She wrote that morning, "Today brings a lot of unknowns to me, but not to You, Lord. You knew about this day (when I was born) fifty-seven years ago. So I pray that the I.V. will go in smoothly. Thanks that I can pray and sing my way through this day." And then, in capital letters, "I LOVE YOU LORD."

That day was so hard for her it nearly drained all her energy. It was so hard that we told our doctor, "No more tests, please, of any kind!"

Mary missed entries for the rest of that week. She was too tired to write. On those exhausted days, our daughters Sara, or Jenn, or one of Mary's sisters would read to her from her devotional books. Then on Friday, May 11, the day after our small group had come over for one of our last meetings together with her, Mary wrote, "I have not had the energy to write anything in my journal but you know all about that, Lord. So today I am writing. I have had a lot of company the last couple of days and feel blessed by them all. Lord, You are still in control. I trust You with the rest of this day."

Her second last entry was Sunday, May 20, before we left for Cobourg to celebrate Mom's 83rd birthday at a family gathering. Mary really got herself "up" for this day and was absolutely thrilled that she could make it. She wrote, "It's been a whole week not writing. Real weakness has set in. So I ask, keep me praying, keep me trusting, every step along life's way. Thank You for this day to celebrate Mom at 83."

The next day she wrote her very last entry. By now it was all she could do to write anything. The writing was actually getting very hard to read. Monday, May 21, 2012, she simply wrote, "Thank you for another day."

When Faith Becomes Noticeable

On the last day of her life, as Mary lay in the hospital, it suddenly became clear that she was dying. She was unable to wake up that day, but it didn't seem like death would happen soon.

I had stepped out for a few moments at noon, and while I was gone Dr. McFadden had come in to check on Mary. I have nothing but good to say about this caring, dedicated family physician. She went way beyond the call of duty for Mary and I'm thankful for her care. Doctors like her are a treasure.

The doctor also wanted to check on me. So she asked the kids to have me come and see her at the nurses' station when I got back. When I arrived, she took me aside, commented on how Mary was doing then turned her full attention to me. Her eyes were measuring me as she asked, "And Bert, how are *you* doing?"

I said I thought I was okay. She asked if I needed anything. Did I need sleeping pills? No, I was able to get to sleep alright last night. Did I need Ativan, or something for my nerves? No; I held out my hand, and it was steady like a rock. I said I thought my nerves were fine.

Then she gave me a quizzical look, like she was trying to figure me out and said, "Your guys' faith is holding you up, isn't it?"

I said, yes, that it was making a real difference for us. She replied, "But that doesn't mean you shouldn't take Ativan, if you need it, does it?"

I think she wanted to be sure my faith wasn't just some kind of smokescreen for denial, a way of escape from the reality of the painful thing that was happening.

So I replied, "No, it doesn't mean I shouldn't take something if I need it. My faith is not about denial. Let me put it to you this way, Doctor. There are different "families" of faith, wouldn't you say? Well in my "family" of faith it's not about pretending something isn't bad when it clearly is. I believe that what's happening to Mary and me right now is awful. It is hurtful, it is painful, it's anything but what's meant to happen to her, it just *sucks*! But I can still be okay, and she can still be okay, because God is still with her, and she still has a future. Our faith says even through all this we can trust Him. So that's what gives us strength. Does that clarify things for you?"

She said, yes it did, and then surprised me by changing the subject. "And Bert, will you do something for me? When this is all over, and you've made funeral arrangements, can you let my office know? I want to be there if I at all possibly can." She gave me a hug, and I went back to Mary's room.

Sometimes you don't think you are ready for something, but you are far more ready than you ever thought was possible.

REFLECTION

1. Which do you think is more instrumental in making a person ready for something like cancer? Is it *believing* the right things or *doing* the right things? Why?

2. Do you think God-followers should somehow be immune to trials, that God owes them a "happily ever after" on this earth? Why is that idea possibly more Disney than Divine?

3. How much difference do you think being "ready" made for Mary? Why?

4. I mentioned physical, emotional, mental and spiritual health. I mentioned a healthy personal devotional life. I mentioned praying (apart and together) and I talked about being part of a healthy church and a healthy small faith-group. Which of those, if any, do you think we would have been fine without?

5. Look again at that list. Make it your list by adding to or deleting from it. What do you think makes a person ready for something like cancer? Now, let me suggest you do something important with your list.

a. First, put a check mark beside the ones that are present in your life right now. Thank God for each of those elements, and think about how you can grow in those areas.

b. Put a question mark beside the ones that are either missing or rather weak in your life right now. Why would it be worth it to change in these areas? How can you actually do it?

4. Making Love: Saying No to Myth and Yes to Truth

When we started out, I believed a number of myths about love and marriage.

Like many young people I wrestled with the notion of "the right one" and whether or not Mary was the one, believing that if she truly was, marriage would be a breeze. I had read a lot of books that talked about a happily-ever-after once you "found" each other, and the common thread in movies and television supported the same idea.

It's the "compatibility" myth. "If you are compatible with one another," the myth goes, "you'll have a good marriage, but if the two of you are not so compatible, you'll have a rocky marriage. It might even be a brief marriage." Mary and I spent a fair bit of energy during our dating years on that question. "Am I sure he is the "right one?" Am I sure she is the "right woman for me?" "Are we really compatible?"

As it turned out, I don't think either compatibility, or being the "right one" had much to do with the good relationship between Mary and me.

In fact, when I look at men and women in general, I sometimes think God must have a sense of humor. He formed us to be attracted to one another. But when we try to live together in marriage, the emphatic differences between a man and a woman easily take center stage and make us angry with each other. Our brains are wired so differently that once we live together, few men and women are all that compatible.

And in addition, there are personality incompatibilities. There certainly were between Mary and me. Let me illustrate. Mary liked things to be neat and tidy. You didn't leave stuff out on the counter even if you were going to use it the very next morning. It was better put away overnight. If you have a clothing drawer, you don't just throw garments in there (even if they fit fine); you fold them and lay them in. Even socks. They are tucked, not tossed.

In many ways this part of her nature was very good for us. I sure could find stuff better when Mary was alive than I can now (surprising, eh?). And our place, even when it was a construction zone, still had a semblance of neatness that made it much more livable. I'm deeply grateful for that part of her personality. But I am not like that by nature. Let's just say I am less-inclined to neatness. Okay -- that's a nice way of saying I am a "messy". My desk is covered with piles as I write this. We were not very compatible in this area. It caused some tension in our marriage right from the very beginning! I mean *right* from the beginning.

A Near-Disaster Honeymoon

It was our wedding night. Mary had changed into her going-away outfit at the reception hall. I stayed in my suit. I seated her in my car, now "our" car (read, my fifth car, pale blue 1967 Rambler American, two-door coupe, straight six with seven main bearings, single carb, naturally aspirated, a fairly plain car, but I kind of liked that one too. It was the "honeymoon" car we drove across Canada a few months later). We waved farewell and were off on our married walk. We were staying the weekend in Huntsville, where I had booked us a motel. We arrived quite late, both very tired from a long day.

I carried her across the threshold. What a silly custom; I nearly smashed her head on the door frame! We were laughing about the close call, enjoying the moment. We entered the room with a lot of happiness, even eagerness on my part. Then I got our stuff inside, locked the door, and was ready for our first night together.

I peeled off my clothes, dropped them, half on a chair and half on the floor, hopped into bed and waited for her. She was being a little slow, I thought. I asked if she was coming. I had not yet been gifted with much patience. And she said yes, she was coming, but she stayed busy putting stuff from her suitcase away, and neatly folding her clothing. As she did, she looked more than once at my clothing-pile. I should have sensed something wasn't quite right, but I wasn't that good at reading her mind yet.

Then she asked me a simple question. "Are you going to hang your clothes up, or are you just going to leave them in a pile like that?" I sensed a bit of tension, but like a dumb ox I said I thought they were okay right where they were. Wrong! She stiffened a bit, her chin came up some, her arms folded, and I heard, "Well then, that's as far as this goes tonight unless you hang them up!" I could tell she meant it. Oh yeah! There could be fire in those beautiful pale-blue eyes!

And there are lots of things I could have said in the surprised incompatibility of that moment. Some of them immediately sprang to my mind. I was always pretty fast with a retort! But something inside me put the brakes on my mouth. It was a crystal clear thought. I'm sure looking back that it was a thought from the Lord. I was a very young Christian at the time, just starting to learn to listen to His promptings. The thought was strong, but not overpowering. It's not like it wasn't optional. The thought was this, "Bert, you know you could make an issue of this right now, but it's probably not worth it, is it?"

I very quickly agreed with the thought and said, "Sorry hon. I didn't know that bothered you. Here, I'll hang them up!" So I did, and that immediately ended the tension. We went to bed and enjoyed the first of many wonderful nights together.

I don't tell you that to make fun of Mary in any way. She wasn't being a nag at all. There was something important going on inside of her. I think she intuitively was *on to something* as a young bride that we didn't actually understand until many years later. I think she knew that for sex to be good for her, and therefore for us, she needed to feel comfortable and cherished, not hurried and used. And she wasn't comfortable with clothes strewn all over the place. It spoke to her of mess and hurry. And it certainly didn't make her feel cherished.

Mary had observed my room at my boyhood home. I always just tossed things in my room at home. If the clothes were okay (understand, "not hideously dirty"), I'd just throw them on a chair, and put them back on in the morning. If I didn't put them back on, I'd leave them on the chair. My mom would gather them and put them in the wash. So intuitively, I think Mary wondered if I would treat my wife like I treated my mother, and that wasn't what she thought a marriage should be. It didn't feel like *cherishing* to her. It felt more like *using*. And it certainly didn't put her in the right frame of mind for making love on our wedding night. Without verbalizing it, I think she just *knew* all that. Over the years I grew to absolutely delight in that intuitive side of Mary. She just knew a lot of stuff I didn't have a clue about.

The point is, that first night together a basic personality incompatibility could have made things go very badly for us, but it didn't. Simple incompatibility could have made it a very bad memory instead of a wonderful memory. And the way we navigated that first night set a tone for the way we began to handle all of our other incompatibilities. Even though I've had to hang up my own clothes ever since, I am so glad it happened like it did!

A Conflict within Conflict

Another incompatibility between Mary and I was in the way we handled conflict. Whenever there was conflict, I was quick to speak and to argue. I actually enjoyed a good argument. It was a challenge, and being from a mostly-boy family, I was used to a lot of that kind of give and take. Mary, however, was anything but like that! Mary's response to conflict was almost always silence, utter and complete silence. She withdrew from conflict. She hated it. It would make her shut down. Her silence would then lead to more anger on my part, which in turn led to more silence. Get the picture? That can go downhill in a hurry.

We discovered very early in our marriage that we could either let these personality differences drive us apart, or we could live together like love mattered more than the difference we were having.

It always boiled down to that kind of choice. And it taught us a strange lesson, namely this. Our incompatibilities, when we choose to embrace them, usually turn out to be strengths. What I was bad at, she was good at! In fact, I remember reading a book once that was built on this very idea. It was called, *Incompatibility, Key to a Great Marriage.* After fifty years of marriage, the author, Chuck Snyder has written a follow-up book called, *Incompatibility: Still Grounds for a Great Marriage.* I'd say he's on to something.

Love Is All You Need

I believed another myth about marriage.

The lyrical prophets of our day, the Beetles, made a lot of coin on the phrase, "Love is all you need," and I believed them. As long as you have love, there isn't really much else you need to have a good and enduring relationship. Everything else will fall into place. Good things will just happen.

Think about it. How many couples do you know who once loved each other but not anymore? If love is all you need, does that mean they never had any love in the first place? I think not. I think many couples who don't make it actually did have love at the start. But love by itself is never enough for a couple to make it through the rough and tumble of married life on planet earth.

Though I started out believing it, we found that whole idea-set to be a myth about marriage. Instead of love being all we needed, we found that love was more like the by-product of a whole bunch of other things that were the *real glue* of marriage.

The Real Glue

We were glued together by our commitment to each other, and by our words to each other. More and more we became each other's best friend. Often we'd say to each other, "You know, I don't only love you, I really *like* you."

We did things together in the evenings. We had no television for the first ten years of our married life, and that was a conscious decision on our part.

The decision was based on observation. When we were engaged, we'd sometimes go for a walk after supper at her house, and often when we came back toward the house, through the window we'd see Mary's family watching the news, or *The Waltons*, or *Hockey Night in Canada*. And we'd stand outside the glass, and watch them watching TV. We found it rather amusing, but also a bit sad. All the eyes are in the same place, and everybody in the same room, but no one is actually connecting with each other.

Everyone is together, but alone. It felt like a "false together". By the way, aren't Facebook and texting the new "false together" in some ways? Doesn't that level of conversation usually leave you feeling a lot less connected than a phone call, and actually hearing someone's tone of voice, or even better, face to face interaction?

Before the beginning of married life we decided we didn't want that kind of *false together* for our home. We wanted our time together to be real, not distracted.

Once married, we made love frequently, sometimes more than once a day and that too bonded us deeply. We were the only sexual partner either one of us ever had, another gift I think. Do you know what effect this had on us? I think it's almost like we "imprinted" on each other. I recently heard the idea that this was one of God's intended purposes when He commanded the exclusivity of sex in marriage. I think I agree.

When "I Love You" isn't the Whole Truth

It was all these kinds of things and more that served as the real glue in our marriage. Love wasn't all we needed. Love grew out of all we needed. I remember saying to Mary after a few years of marriage, "You know how I used to say, 'I love you,' when we first were married? I'm sorry. I didn't mean to, but I lied to you. I thought it was love, but I now realize it wasn't love. I didn't love you, I liked you a lot. *Now* I love you." And she'd say the same thing. As three decades rolled by, we were still saying similar words to each other. Only now it was, "I really did love you then, but I love you even more now!"

Enjoy it While You are Young

There is another myth I believed about love: Enjoy the passion while you are young, because older people inevitably lose it. That's just the way it is! When observing people our parents' age, they just didn't seem to be physically affectionate. They didn't seem to kiss, other than on the cheek, or in a perfunctory way. Oh, I know back then older people had this "thing" about not showing affection in public. But it seemed to be more than that. They didn't seem to be attracted to each other.

Thankfully, I discovered that this, too, was just a myth. Mary and I lived out the truth that no part of love ever has to get stale and old. I used to tell Mary that I looked forward to making love with her on her 80th birthday. She'd just smile, and say, "We'll see about that!" But there would always be that twinkle in her eye. The fact is, Mary and I had as much real attraction and passion for one another in our 37th year as we had in any year of our marriage.

Even after cancer we passionately enjoyed each other. I was afraid to at first, so we agreed to experiment, making sure what we were doing wasn't hurting her. The deal was that she could say the word and we would immediately stop. More gently and carefully than before cancer, intimacy was a gift we kept giving to each other until the last weeks of her life.

By then, she was actually surprised I would find her attractive. She even said to me one time, "Oh, hon, do you still want me that way?" Her mirror was telling her that cancer was bloating her abdomen while at the same time leaving almost no flesh on other parts of her body. She didn't feel attractive any more. I told her she was still the most beautiful woman on earth to me, both in body and in spirit. I told her I would always want her that way. Cancer actually made both of us want each other more. Each time we made love, we wondered if it might be the last time we would enjoy each other.

You Don't Have to Say "Sorry"

It was a pretty commonly held belief back then that if you had true love, you would automatically understand and forgive when there were hurts or offences. Love meant never having to say you were sorry. I think that's how it was put. I actually believed that myth.

It wasn't helped by the Dutch-Canadian subculture which we both grew up in. A few years ago someone pointed out to me that the Dutch vocabulary does not include the word, "sorry." They have words like "I feel regret," or "I am sad about that," and the like, but not the actual apology, "I am sorry." That might explain why I never recall hearing that Dutch word. I'm not sure if the observation is true or not, but I do know that when we were first married, the words, "I'm sorry," were not really a very conscious part of my vocabulary. The first time I had to say those words to Mary, it was like pulling my own teeth without painkillers. But the pain of silence between us felt worse than not apologizing.

Mary found it very difficult to apologize, too. But we soon discovered something. While both of us would have to talk ourselves into an apology, as soon as we did, it was worth it! It is so good to live in a forgiven state. Both of us were capable of hurting each other, but neither of us held on to the hurts. Instead of never having to say we were sorry, we became good at quickly saying it, then simply forgiving each other, and moving on from there. I mean really moving on. Once something was forgiven, it was never brought up again.

So don't believe everything you think you know about love. There are a lot of myths concerning love and marriage. The sooner you stop believing the myths and start practicing the truth, the better your love-walk will be.

REFLECTION

1. Do you think our culture believes the compatibility myth? What evidence would support your answer?

2. What gender-fueled incompatibilities have caused stress in your relationship? How specifically could they be used to bless your relationship instead of harm it?

3. What personality-based incompatibilities have caused stress in your relationship? How could they be used to bless instead of harm the relationship?

4. What do you think is the difference between *false* time spent together in a relationship and *quality* time spent together? Does your relationship major on false or quality together-time?

5. In Proverbs 5:15-18 the Bible encourages the exclusivity of married love. It says, "15. Drink

water from your own cistern, running water from your own well. 16. Should your springs overflow in the streets, your streams of water in the public squares? 17. Let them be yours alone, never to be shared with strangers. 18. May your fountain be blessed and *may you rejoice in the wife of your youth."* (emphasis mine) What are you specifically doing to protect:

a. the reality of that exclusivity?

b. the joy of that exclusivity?

6. Proverbs 5:18 goes on to talk about the joy of a life-long sexual relationship between husband and wife.

"A loving doe, a graceful deer- may her breasts satisfy you always, may you ever be intoxicated with her love." How does this verse counteract the "better enjoy it while you are young" myth?

7. Think of the following decision: "I'd sooner love you than fight with you." If you really decided that, what effect would the decision have?

a. on your ability to apologize?

b. on your ability to forgive?

c. on your ability to forget what the fights were about?

8. What other things have you discovered to be myths when it comes to growing a lasting love?

5. Learning Mary

The pace of our marriage's growth remained fairly slow until something important began to happen. I began to *learn* Mary. I began to know *her*.

It wasn't something I had planned to do. But I began to obey 1 Peter 3:7, which is one of those scriptures directed specially to husbands. It says, "Husbands, in the same way be considerate as you live with your wives, and treat them with respect as the weaker partner." The word translated as "considerate" is more literally, "according to knowledge."

The single word we translate "live with" is more profound in the Greek than we might realize. One commentator I read actually calls it, "ultimate profundity." The word is talking about three levels of living together all at once. It is profound because it links together in one word, at least two levels of living together *now*, in the context of our final living together in *eternity*.

What are the two levels of living together *now*? On one level it is talking about our "everyday" living together. We get up, make the bed together, do the dishes, have a conversation, make a decision, wash the car, buy groceries, and go for a walk and so on. We do a lot of mundane, ordinary things in our living together. What we translate, "live with," is talking about these everyday things.

But that is not all it is referring to. While talking about those everyday things, it is actually intending to allude at the same time to the "physical marriage relationship." It is talking also about our sexual union.

Both of those levels are in view at the same time here. Peter is not talking about one or the other. He is talking simultaneously about both.

Peter is addressing those two levels of our relationship within the framework of a third level of relationship, that of our future inheritance, our eternal living together. So this verse is talking about our "everyday living together" and "making love together" as we "move to eternity together."

This verse is telling me that as a husband, God wants me to live with my wife in an "understanding way", in every part of our living together, from doing the dishes, to keeping the finances, to making love, and also to live in an understanding way with her as someone who is to share with me in eternal life, and to recognize that in many ways, our "living together" is part of preparing us for that greater future, when our love will be raised to perfection[3]. Wow!

In all of this, the husband in particular is told to live together with his wife "according to knowledge."

---

[3] It will be perfect love, even though it will no longer be as husband and wife. Must be some love!

The Subject of a Husband's Knowing

An important question to ask ourselves is this, "According to *what* knowledge?" According to biblical knowledge? According to the knowledge of God? While those are good, that is not what Peter has in mind here. He has something else in mind. In this verse, our *wives* are the object of our "living together in an understanding way". The verse is saying a husband is not to just understand God and God's commands. He is not just to understand life and how life works, or even to have a clear understanding of himself, knowing what *he* wants out of life and marriage. He is to understand his *wife* and the inner workings of his *wife*.

It is *her* he is to understand, in every area of their life together, from dishes, to shopping, to children, to walking, to entertainment, to sex, to the way she responds to God in worship. What does she like, and what doesn't she (from socks to symphonies)? What turns her off and makes it hard to give herself to me sexually, and what turns her on? What is her spiritual learning style? What is her worship style?

Why do you think the Bible gives husbands that command, not wives? Why isn't this one of those "each other" commands? Probably because most husbands *need* the command, and most of our wives don't, so much. Mary could have answered the majority of those questions about me after a year of marriage. Of course, she grew in this area too, but it was me that really needed to grow in my understanding of her. If our marriage was to move from minor league to major league, I would need to make the cut in this area. I needed to get to know Mary.

My "knowing her" was foundational in the area of our getting along with each other as well as we did. "Knowing her" made all the difference in allowing both of us to enjoy a lifetime together of wonderful sex. "Knowing her" was integral to us being on the same page spiritually, complementing each other in our walk with God and in our worship and our prayers, instead of getting in each other's way. I got to *know* Mary, and it was good.

Becoming a Knowledge Ace

Three things happened between Mary and me that helped me to improve at "living according to knowledge" with her.

First, we talked a lot. Not, *she* talked a lot. *We* talked a lot. That is of no small importance to a thriving marriage. We talked a lot.

Keep in mind, the first ten years of our marriage we had no television. I'd come home from work, play with the kids while she finished making supper; we'd eat as a family sitting around the table, work together at cleaning up (no dishwasher), play together with the kids some more and read to them, put them to bed *early* (good for them and good for us), and have about two hours together almost every night to have a coffee, hang out together, and just talk about my day and her day and the kids and the extended family and anything else. Or if I was working on the house that evening (it took me almost ten years to finish "chinking" the log house, our first home), she'd usually be in there helping, and we'd talk as I worked. All this everyday talk was very important to my "knowing" her.

We didn't stop talking at the bedroom door. I risked my male ego to "ask" her things about sex. Really, think about it! Isn't it downright stupid of us men to have an ego in this area, as if we are supposed to be born good at it or something?

I've got to be honest here. In the first year or two of our marriage I'd ask Mary, "Was that good for you?" But I wasn't really asking. I was actually looking for affirmation more than what she honestly liked. And she could sense that, so the standard answer was always, "Yea, hon that was great!"

It wasn't until a few years later that the questions started to become honest. It wasn't until I became truly interested in what pleased her as much as what pleased me, that the questions became real. The questions started to become more specific and less general. Instead of "Was that good for you?" it became "What part of that was best for you? Mary, I love your pleasure as much as mine. Knowing you are turned on is my biggest turn-on. So let's talk each other through sex. Tell me when something is good for you, and please tell me when we need to change it up."

It involved a bit of a risk but it built a lot of trust, and became fun for us. It would not have been so if we had not talked a lot. It was absolutely foundational in the early years, and became very important again in the last year, when cancer entered our everyday lives, and the bedroom too.

Our First Book

The second thing that made a huge difference for us in this whole knowledge department happened during our first winter of marriage. My mom gave us a Christian book on marriage and family. It was the first book we had that wasn't mine or Mary's. Rather, it was ours. Since we were expecting our first child, we thought we'd better read it. So that fall and winter, we would read it together most days. We did it at the close of the day, as we lay side by side on our bed. I'd read a paragraph, then she'd read a paragraph, and we'd talk about what it said. We went through it slowly, a few pages at a time. We were eager to learn.

That book became foundational for us. It was called, *The Christian Family* (1970, Minneapolis, Bethany Fellowship). Our attitude in reading that book was very simple. We were young. So to us everything was black and white. Whatever we saw in the book that struck us as being true to the Bible, we would just do it that way. It wouldn't be me telling her to do it, or her trying to convince me to do it. I wasn't lord, and she wasn't nag. There was no manipulation and no pressure. We'd both just do it by the book. That was our shared agreement from the start. We owed much of our early success in marriage to that book.

A third thing which helped me to understand Mary occurred while I was studying at Central Baptist Seminary and Bible College, Toronto, from 1982 to 1987. When I started we had been married seven years. The school was concerned about pressures that could be placed on the families of their graduates, so they organized two seminars for married couples in the years of my schooling. Mary and I attended both of these retreats. They were the first marriage seminars we ever attended. And they were helpful. It was another bump up in the knowledge department for me. It made an impact on us, but an even greater ramping up of my knowledge of Mary was just around the corner.

Live-Saver Reading

In 1987 I began serving as the pastor of a local church, and suddenly had people coming to me for counselling in regards to their marriages. I realized I had so much to learn in this area before I could be of real help to them. Fortunately, the church library had about ten very good books on marriage. I bought another ten. I read them all with a "save my ministry life" attitude. Did I ever learn a lot about marriage in a short time! There was a side benefit to all this reading. It not only showed me how to help other people's marriages; it profoundly impacted my own. It helped me to understand Mary in a whole new way.

It is interesting that those books came into our lives right around the time that is often referred to as "the ten-year itch." We'd been married for ten years, yes, but for us it was anything but boring. Instead, we were learning new things that kept our marriage fresh and interesting, fascinating, even! The more I learned about Mary, the more interesting she became to me.

And then we started doing pre-marital counselling. And that led to more books, and more learning. I just kept buying books. By the time I gave a bunch of them away last year to a pastor just starting out, I had well over fifty books on marriage. It became my practice to purchase and read a least one new book on marriage every year. For us it was like attending our own annual marriage seminar.

Marriage-Builder Reading

Here's how it worked for us. I learn best from reading. Mary learned best by talking. I'd read, then Mary and I would talk. Then we would re-enforce what we learned by doing it.

Even in the last year of our marriage, we were still growing in the knowledge department. Our small group was studying a book about marriage. And we became aware of gender differences we had never known before.

That's the way it was for us through our entire married life. We were always learning something new and fresh. It was so worth it.

So, to those husbands out there, please never stop learning about your wife. I know for some of you, reading is not your learning style. So then *what is* your learning style? And what resources suited to your learning style are available? Is it a men's group? Is it being one-on-one with a trusted friend who can talk to you about marriage? Is it a video series? Is it taking your wife to a marriage retreat every year? Whatever it is, I suggest you find what suits you, and make sure you do it.

The Apostle Peter was on to something when he wrote that command to husbands. Love grows where there is knowledge. There is a direct relationship between the growth of knowledge and the growth of marriage. May you never get to thinking you know "enough already!"

Learning Mary was one of the best and most pleasurable things I ever did.

REFLECTION

For Husbands

1. Recall the excitement you felt when you first met and got to know your wife. Wasn't she fascinating? Has the fascination...

    a. grown?

    b. stayed the same?

    c. ebbed?

    d. gone?

2. What can you do to change things for the good in this area?

3. How much do you talk with your wife about the intimacy you share? (Monosyllables don't count)

4. If you'd like to go further in this thing of knowing her, how would a plan help? How would talking the plan over with her be helpful?

5. Have you ever asked your wife if there are things she is afraid to talk to you about? Why is that a fairly important question? What should you do if you are not sure her answer is honest?

For Wives

1. How do you suppose the way men and women think very differently make this command harder for your husband to keep?

2. Your responsiveness can either encourage your husband to really know you, or slam the door in his face. In what ways have you...

> a. been a happy encourager in this area?

> b. let him learn you if he really wants?

> c. made it somewhat difficult for him?

> c. slammed doors?

3. In what way does it feel risky to let your husband know "too much"? What does power have to do with it?

6. Learning Cancer

Until Mary was diagnosed, I knew very little about cancer. I never thought about it much, and I didn't want to.

Who gets cancer? If pressed, I'd have said maybe those who have a genetic predisposition. If not genetics, I might have mentioned exposure to asbestos or radiation, whether from too much sun, radon gas, ex-rays and so on. So how much is too much of any of these? I don't know, I think there are legal limits.

What if I or someone I love was actually diagnosed with cancer? What could we do? What treatments work? Does the stage of cancer matter? Does the type of cancer matter? If you'd asked me those questions, the answers would have been tentative. I think stage goes by numbers, and I think a higher number is worse. Or perhaps it's the other way around? Not sure what the numbers mean.

What treatments work? Well, my brother-in-law had leukemia, and although chemo nearly killed him, he's in remission today. And my mother-in-law had breast cancer and the combination of surgery and radiation seemed to do wonders for her. Neither of those cancers had metastasized. But wait, Mary's cousin had cancer years ago, and I remember she refused her doctor's treatments, and went with what they called "natural" treatments instead. So what was that? I don't know, I never really asked.

A Naive Kind of Hope

I had a naive kind of hope when it comes to cancer. Aren't they making big strides in fighting it? The surgery is getting much more precise and dependable isn't it? And the radiation is getting much more accurate. And chemo has improved a lot too, no?

Shortly after Mary's diagnosis, one of her sisters was talking to a friend who was a doctor. "Tell Mary not to worry," the doctor said. "They can do so much more these days than they used to." After the billions we've spent on fighting cancer, surely we *are* further ahead are we not? Doesn't success usually follow money?

That was me when we heard those life-changing words, "So Mary, about your cancer."

We immediately began a medical journey nobody wants to go on. Mary had been booked for surgery in two weeks. In a few days we were at the surgeon's office for her pre-op. It was the usual stuff about getting ready for surgery. But I was surprised by some unusual advice the surgeon gave us as well. He looked at me with a little grin and said, "And listen, the internet is good for porn, but not for cancer." Believing all porn is degrading exploitation at best, I was a little annoyed. But I bit my tongue, not quite sure I had heard him correctly. I had. Before we left, he repeated the little pearl of wisdom.

Mary and I talked about it on the way home, wondering where that statement came from. We decided he was purposely trying to shock us to make a strong point, the point being, "If you want answers about cancer, do *not* get them from the internet. It is nothing but a cesspool of misinformation when it comes to cancer." If that's what he meant, he probably should have just said that, as well as given us the names of some sites that were not full of misinformation.

It was a moot point. I was still too stunned by the diagnosis to do much reading anyways. Then surgery brought bad news. Things were far worse than we had hoped. It wasn't just a tumor. The surgeon had taken biopsies from lymph nodes and the fatty layer around Mary's organs (omentum). He had felt at least six tumors on Mary's liver. One of them was the size of a small orange. I had no idea how much worse that actually was.

Two weeks later we were again in his office, getting the results of the biopsies. They were all malignant except some of the lymph nodes. I knew that wasn't good, but I still had a naive kind of hopefulness.

We asked about the prognosis. He said her cancer was treatable but not curable. That sounded hopeful. Then he said treatment would be palliative. That felt like a gut shot. To me it meant, "Keep her comfortable as she dies." It was the first rending of my naive hope in modern medicine.

He said treatment wouldn't be too bad, like chemo-lite, not too many side effects. If she responded well, most people with Mary's stage of cancer live one to three years. If she did not respond well, it could be three months. The conversation didn't dwell on time. He just mentioned it and we were left digesting it. I didn't hear much after the three months part. He was referring us to cancer specialists and wished us well. Any questions? None seemed to come to mind, so we left for home.

An Education Begins

As we were driving home I did think of some questions. What exactly was *palliative* treatment? How did it differ from other treatment? Doesn't chemo make you highly uncomfortable? How can it be palliative then? And more importantly, was there anything we could do to help treatments be effective? Was there a difference we could make? Was there anything we could do to help Mary be on the long end of time, not the short?

Those questions were the beginning of a cancer education for me. I got on the steepest learning curve of my life. I began to search out everything I could about cancer. If there was even one little thing we could do to help Mary, I wanted to know about it.

I pushed past the surgeon's warning and began to search the internet for information. After all, there *had* to be lots of good information there, even if there would be bad. It's like that with everything on the web. The key is *discerning* the good from the bad. So I started with what I thought would probably be a very accurate site, the Mayo Clinic in the USA.

I began by exploring what the stages of cancer meant. I found out that staging is an assessment of the spread of the cancer. Though there is more than one way of staging, spread is often gauged by numbers, from one to four.

One means the earliest, most treatable stage of cancer. In stage two, the cancer has just begun to spread from its local containment. In three it has gone to surrounding lymph nodes, and four, the worst, it has spread to distant organs. The more I read, the more serious my thoughts became. I realized Mary's cancer was not just stage four, but advanced stage four, with multiple tumors in distant organs. It was at the bottom of the chart, no matter which chart I was looking at.

Panic Hits Home

I then flipped to another chart that gave the prognosis for survival by stage. Panic hit. In an instant I lost what was left of my naive hope. It seems the surgeon had been *much more* than optimistic. According to the chart, my remaining time with Mary was going to be a lot shorter than he had said. Inoperable metastasis to liver meant months at most. Panic laid a strong grip on my stomach. I could feel it rise and begin to grasp my lungs. I could hardly breathe. I had to look away from the screen, close my eyes, grip the desk and just pray.

As prayer began to overcome panic, a sentence played across my mind. "Looks like we're down to our last hope," I thought. I reflected on that for a few seconds and then rephrased it, still praying. "No Lord," I breathed, "That's not really true is it? Actually, we're up to our first hope." I had a strong feeling that the only real hope we had was in God's intervention.

That thought wasn't my new naive. It was a reality check. And I never again felt a hint of panic.

Instead of panic, there was determination. I put the numbers in front of me aside. The crucial question was still unanswered. Was there anything we could do to help Mary? I wiped my tears and went back to the screen. I went back with attitude. My game face was on. I went to work for Mary.

Doctor-Death or Snake-Oil?

The next week or so I spent hours and hours looking for answers on the internet. As I began to widen my search, I found a confusing mass of information. The range was incredible, all the way from, "There's nothing you can do except manage pain and symptoms," to "the overnight cure for all cancers." And that was after weeding out sites that seemed bizarre. Where, between the extremes, was the truth?

The rhetoric I found was even worse. On one end of the scale I found seemingly rational people saying, "Chemotherapy is nothing but assisted suicide." On the polar opposite, "anything but chemotherapy is nothing but quackery." Was everything either "doctor death" or "snake-oil?" What then, could I trust? Maybe this is what the doctor meant when he warned me about the internet?

The contradictions didn't stop me from searching, just made me wary. What could we do to help Mary? That question became my new normal. Love was driving me to find the answers.

A Chance Conversation

A few days later we had a chance conversation with my sister Judy and her husband, Andy. He was in his fourth year of remission from Leukemia. They told us about their experiences at Sunnybrook, a major cancer center in Toronto. Their oncologist had recommended that along with chemotherapy they adopt an anti-cancer diet for Andy.

They loaned us a book their specialist had recommended, written by two researchers in molecular medicine in Montreal. It was called,

Foods That Fight Cancer[4]. Within a few hours I had devoured it. That was the first time I'd heard, from a scientific source, that foods make a difference in both preventing and fighting cancer. Could there actually be an anti-cancer diet even after you had cancer?

---

[4] *Foods That Fight Cancer*, Richard Beliveau and Denis Gingras, Toronto, Mclelland & Stewart, 2006. The authors are leading authorities on cancer research at the University of Quebec, in Montreal. Highlights of the book:

-about 1/3 of all cancers are directly related to diet

-three to four servings of broccoli per week is enough to protect you from colon polyps.

-all cruciferous vegetables (Brussels sprouts, broccoli, cabbage, cauliflower, kale) lightly cooked and thoroughly chewed have anti-cancer effects

-curcumin inhibits and prevents colon cancer (a teaspoon of turmeric per day added to soups, dressings or pasta dishes is enough)

-green tea contains catechins that fight cancer. The best green tea is Japanese, brewed at least 8 minutes, and consumed fresh (better than from a thermos).

-citrus fruits are essential in cancer prevention.

-ginger has anti-inflammatory compounds that fight cancer and other chronic inflammatory diseases

-(I liked this one, I liked it a lot!) consuming 40 grams of dark chocolate (70% cocoa) has definite benefits.

-instead of replacing butter with margarine, use olive oil as much as possible. The book was well laid out, colourful, well documented, full of practical information, a real eye opener .

Apparently the idea was either controversial or unknown to the medical professionals helping Mary. After reading about foods making a difference, I began asking our doctors and nurses at the cancer center what Mary should be eating to help fight cancer. Was there anything in diet that would help in her situation?

The whole idea was quickly brushed off by every doctor or nurse I asked. It was treated with disdain. They made us feel like anything beyond the four walls of chemotherapy was quackery. Our oncologist answered by referring us to a staff dietician. I was hopeful as she came into the room, eager for specific dietary advice geared to Mary's condition and stage of disease, but her only advice was, "Be sure to eat a balanced diet from the four food groups," and "there may come a time when you need extra calories, so take as many sugars and fats and carbs and proteins as you can. Do all you can to keep your weight up. These products (she gave us some samples of meal replacements) will be sure to help you and they come in so many more flavors now."

According to what I had just read, that isn't *real* help. That's loading up on a diet that fuels cancer while ignoring the specific needs a body has when fighting cancer. It was the first time I seriously wondered, "Given all you *do* know within these four walls of chemotherapy, what *don't* you know?"

I went back to the internet. I was discovering that the difference of opinion on diet was just the tip of the iceberg. Disagreement was everywhere about almost everything. It didn't matter if I was searching *alternative* sites or *traditional* sites or reading from journals of oncology. What one oncologist said would help, another oncologist said would hurt. What one alternative site recommended, another alternative site discounted.

I Needed a Foundation

I realized I needed something of a foundation from which to judge what I read. So as a starting point, I went back to a basic tenet of my own worldview. I reminded myself that God has created a stable earth, one governed by laws of nature which He has ordained.[5] Those laws were foundational even to cancer treatments. If there was something we could do to help Mary, it should be verifiable and explainable. Any treatment should make sense to me. It should be more

---

[5] I believe He is nevertheless involved actively and personally. He can and does choose to make an exception to the laws (a miracle), but he usually doesn't. A miracle remains a miracle, not a normal event. There would be no such thing as a miracle if His intervention were the norm. If miracles were the new norm, then non-intervention would be the new miracle. So instead of praising God, a belief in miracle as "normative" is not praising Him at all, because a lot of us obviously don't get a miracle. If miracle is normal, the disappointment we see in life means God is cruel at best, and your Christianity is rather cruel too. It becomes sub-Christian, not super-Christian to believe in miracle as norm. The norm is the rule of the natural laws He Himself has designed.

scientific than mysterious, even if I couldn't necessarily explain everything about it. I am not a chemist, and we are after all, fearfully and wonderfully made. But treatments should be sensible.

That reminder in place, I faced a trust question. Whose writing then, could I believe in? Time being critical, how could I cut to the chase and find authors who were trustworthy?

In a lifetime of reading, I have usually found authors with a balanced Christian worldview are pulled toward truth. If an author actually believes in the God of truth it leads to a desire to write truthfully. That doesn't mean I blindly believe everything written by a Christian author. I've read some weird ones. I just feel I have a better chance if pressed for time, of finding truth when reading a Christian author.

So I decided to begin to build a foundation of cancer knowledge by reading ten Christian authors on cancer. I've read lots of non-Christian writers since. But for time's sake, I began with Christian authors. I was surprised to discover many hundreds were in print. Books ranged from medical to experiential to theological. I chose from each category, ordered books and waited for them eagerly.

They came on a Thursday and by the end of that weekend I had done a quick read of them all. I settled in to give more focussed attention to five of them. I began with two testimonial books.

Meet Anne Frahm

First I read Anne Frahm's, *A Cancer Battle Plan*[6]. Her breast cancer spread to her lungs and bones. She endured every conventional therapy; surgery, chemotherapy, radiation and hormone therapy, then finally a harrowing bone marrow transplant. She was often near death. Everything failed to send her cancer into remission. She was told there was nothing more that could be done. Hers was a hopeless case.

---

[6] A Cancer Battle Plan, Anne E. and David J. Frahm, New York, N.Y., Penguin Putnam Inc., 1997. There are six principles in the book. One: Know Your Enemy (how cancer thrives). Two: Cut off Enemy Supply Lines. Frahm believes that dietary fat and protein from animal products are major cancer promoters. At the same time, the liver and bowel must be detoxified and functioning well. Three: Rebuild Your Natural Defense System. Here Frahm emphasises the role of live foods (not over-cooked or processed) in supplying the enzymes your immune system needs to function properly. Exercise has a positive effect on the immune system as well. Four: Bring In Re-enforcements. Nearly all cancer patients have vitamin and mineral deficiencies, made worse by the disease. This must be rectified to give the body the opportunity to heal. Five: Maintain Morale. There must be a fighting spirit, one that takes charge of one's own health, refuses to play victim, lives thankfully, finds humor every day, and sets goals to achieve. Six: Carefully Select Your Professional Help. Frahm suggests a cancer patient needs a team of professionals helping fight the disease. An oncologist to monitor the disease and help beat down cancer at crucial times and a Nutritionist (not dietician) who can test and guide in the specific nutrients needed by the patient. A Metabolic Physician is also needed to assess the biochemical needs of the body, and address deficiencies intravenously if necessary. Finally, a Chiropractor to address the needs of the nervous system.

Having nothing left to lose, she began a strict regimen of detoxification, diet and supplements. Five weeks later, tests by her oncologist revealed no trace of cancer.

The book strongly affirmed to me that Mary's case was not hopeless. Anne's cancer was more advanced than Mary's. Yet Anne had come back to being cancer free. Why couldn't Mary?

Second, her book strongly suggested that there was real help outside the four walls of chemotherapy. At first I found that hard to believe, but through her book I began to think that there was possibly something Mary could do to make a difference.

Though she was labelled a hopeless case, Anne lived many cancer-free years. That made a strong impression on me.

Say Hello to Larry Burkett

Next I read Larry Burkett's, *Nothing to Fear*[7]. I chose his book because I had read other works by Burkett. I knew he was a no-nonsense, down to earth guy. I could probably trust what he wrote simply because of the kind of person and researcher I knew he was. In other books that I had read, he wrote believable stuff.

Larry chronicles his own experience with kidney cancer that spread to his shoulder blade, then later to his other kidney and beyond. Almost no one survives that. His book is short, direct, easy reading and outlines Larry's journey through both traditional and non traditional therapies. I found some very strong chapters in his book on how faith overcomes fear and on maintaining hope. Chapter 5 on the role of alternative medicine was particularly helpful.

Overall, Larry's book was very logical and persuasive. A lot of what he said dovetailed with what Anne had said. Again, I was left with a fairly powerful question. If these kinds of treatments worked for Larry and Anne, why couldn't they work for Mary?

Having read two testimonial books, I decided to focus on three books written by medical people. One was by a naturopathic doctor, one by a surgical oncologist, the final by a psychologist.

[7] Larry Burkett, *Nothing to Fear, The Key to Cancer Survival*, Chicago, Illinois, Moody Press, 2003. Larry has written what he calls a "crash course" on cancer survival. He begins by encouraging a patient to aggressively seek the best treatment they can from the doctors who have the best success rates. He reminds us that traditional treatments can be very dangerous (most cancer patients die from complications as a result of treatments), and that not all alternative treatments are shams. Larry learned to live with cancer, but without worry or fear. Chapter 2 is called, *Faith Versus Fear*. Fear is our normal response to cancer.. Larry strongly urges us to get to know God so that we can banish fear. To him, this makes spiritual sense, but it also makes practical sense. Fear and anxiety suppress your immune system, while laughter, joy and calm relaxation boost it. Chapter 3 discusses Larry's treatment decisions. He went to Prague for immune therapy, changed to a mostly vegetarian diet, increased his level of exercise, drank ozonated water, had T-cell stimulation therapy, cryogenic ablation as well as radiofrequency ablation. Chapter 4 is about the role of nutrition. Larry had a complete nutritional analysis done on his hair, blood, urine and saliva. They revealed deficiencies in basic minerals and vitamins as well as higher than acceptable levels of mercury and lead in his system. He had all his amalgam fillings removed and replaced with ceramics, then went on a one-year regimen of 12 grams of Chlorella per day (as per a Harvard Medical School Study he had found) to cleanse his body of heavy metals. Chapter 5 is on the role of alternative therapies. It is a good discussion of the way traditional and alternative medicines are usually opposed to one another. Larry respectfully asks both to be more accepting of one another. He believes he's alive long after he should have been dead because of both arms of medicine. The chapter has a helpful section on how he screens alternative therapies. He applies the rules to traditional therapies as well. 1. Discernment: Larry only accepts a therapy if it is performed by someone with an earned degree in the science administered. 2. Verifiable statistics: Larry demands them for both treatments and supplements. 3. Verifiable therapies: he first assesses the harm the therapy may cause, and always refuses to be the first to try it. 4. Reasonable cost: it's user-pay. 5. Nothing bizarre: 6. Independent testing: assess the effectiveness of the therapy by traditional tests. Chapter 6 is about being peaceful, not passive and contains 11 practical suggestions on how exactly to do that. Chapters 7 and 8 follow with teaching on how to maintain hope and wisdom. His thoughts about peace, hope and wisdom are Larry's main reason for writing.

A Naturopathic Doctor Writes

John A Catanzaro[8] advocates for what he
calls an integrative approach in his book. He warns

---

[8] John A Catanzaro, *Cancer, an Integrative Approach*, Enumclaw,
WA, Winepress Publishing, 2004. Chapters 1-3 argue that a cancer
patient does best when both traditional and alternative therapies are
blended. Chapter 4 is a good primer on cancer, especially its causes
and prevention. Chapter 5 lists the major types of cancer, their
diagnoses, staging and the types of treatment being used, both
traditional and alternative. The next chapter describes the 19 most
common cancer detection tests, closing with a summary of what tests
should be performed at what stages. Chapter 7 outlines
conventional treatments, including side effects of chemotherapy and
radiation. Chapter 8 is about biological therapy and alternative
immunotherapy. These are designed to enhance the body's own
immune system against cancer function. Chapters 9 and 10 discuss
hormone replacement therapies and intravenous chelation and
nutritional therapies. 11 is about nutritional and diet therapies. It
discusses five key anti-oxidants in cancer prevention and control,
vitamins A, C and E, Selenium and C0Q10, then 27 key nutrients
including Beta carotene, Omega 3,6 and 9 fatty acids, probiotics and
water. There is a good discussion of problems people have had with
some diet therapies. Chapter 12 outlines 22 herbs used in cancer
treatment including a description of their effects and common
dosages. The next chapter is a survey of common alternative
treatment options, as well as a brief assessment of Cancer Clinics in
Mexico and outside the USA. Chapter 14 is overtly Christian,
emphasising the need to be healed in our relationship with God and
man, and live in peace and true purpose, free from worry. It has
some good suggestions on developing a worry list, a prayer list and
an action list. Chapter 15 contains case histories of five individuals
Catanzaro has helped through cancer, one with breast cancer,
another with lung cancer (mets to brain), a third with prostate, the
fourth with multiple myeloma and the final, bladder cancer. Three are
cancer free as of writing date, two outlived their original prognosis.
The final chapter has a conclusion and helpful cancer resources
including web sites.

---

against looking for a single isolated cause and cure for cancer. Instead of deciding *between* traditional or alternative medicine, his integrative approach aims to *unify* the two healing systems, blending the best of both in the fight against cancer. His book is really a reference guide to the kinds of treatments being offered, both traditional and alternative, with hints on how to blend them. He covers a vast array of subjects. The Table of Contents alone is ten pages long.

After reading this book, it began to serve as a reference work for me. From then on, whenever I read of a treatment or test I had a good idea of what it was talking about. A foundation of knowledge was gradually being built.

Dr. Contreras and a Mexican Perspective

Dr. Francisco Contreras is a second-generation surgeon and oncologist. His book[9] begins with five chapters that discuss causes and characteristics of cancer. He then outlines twenty natural, spiritual and medicinal remedies that can slow down or even reverse cancer growth.

This book too made a strong impression on me. I would have loved to take Mary to South California or Mexico to the Oasis of Hope cancer treatment centres. The combining of traditional and alternative therapies seemed to make sense. But Mary didn't want to go that far away from family. It felt like giving up her life to try to find life. So instead, I began to look for ways to do the things I had been reading about from home, and trying to find people who practiced the kinds of therapies that would be helpful alongside chemotherapy.

Some of you might be thinking, "Poor you, Bert. I know what's going on here. If you look hard enough, you find what you *want* to find. I feel a bit sorry for you. You are just setting yourself up for major disappointment. Don't you know that all alternative cancer treatment is just driven by money?"

I might have said that myself a few years ago. In fact I've never even been to a chiropractor. I didn't even trust *that* branch of alternative medicine (if it's alternative). This isn't a case of me

[9] Franscisco Contreras and Daniel Kennedy, *Beating Cancer, 20 Natural, Spiritual & Medicinal Remedies*, Lake Mary, Florida, Siloam, 2010. Chapters 1-3 discuss the challenge of fighting cancer, arguing for a paradigm shift. We need to stop looking for a magic bullet, doing every little thing we know of against cancer instead. Next he summarizes how cancer fights. Chapter 5 discusses chemotherapy, radiation and surgery, their strengths as well as their limitations. The three have an overall failure rate because of the false premise that the *tumor* is the *disease*. In reality, it is the symptom. We need to restore the organic deficiency that led to the tumor. That is why Contreras is committed to offering other therapies alongside them. Section two of the book outlines 20 such therapies. Chapter 6 considers the first 4. In Ozone Therapy, ozone in the blood produces a higher level of hydrogen peroxide, which increases the delivery of oxygen (works against cancer, for normal cells) and inhibits angiogenesis (formation of new blood cells) on which cancer thrives. At the same time it stimulates the body's own immune system. In Ultraviolet Light Therapy the patient's own blood is drawn and exposed to U.V. light, then re-infused. This stimulates the immune system as well. The 3rd therapy, melatonin, inhibits cancer cells while stimulating proper gene expression. In the 4th, Lymphocyte Therapy, a patient is infused with lymphocytes (white blood cells involved in immune defence) from a young, healthy, unrelated donor. This activates dendridic (immune)cells. In chapter 7 Contreras introduces dietary, environmental, genetic and viral factors that promote cancer. He elaborates on these in chapters 8-10. First he says a nutritionally deficient and toxin laden diet is a major cancer promoter. In addition, caffeine, nicotine, alcohol, artificial sweeteners and prescription drugs burden the immune system. In chapter 8 he suggests the Mediterranean Diet (high in olive oil, legumes, whole grains, fruits, vegetables, tomatoes, grapes and nuts, but low in meat and dairy. This diet has an antioxidant and an anti-inflammatory effect. Similarly the Hallelujah Diet tries to rectify nutrient deficiency and toxicity by emphasising raw and preferably organic foods. Dr. Joel Fuhrman in *Eat to Live* emphasises the same things. The chapter closes by summarizing other cancer-fighting foods, tomatoes (lycopene), olive oil (high monounsaturated/ saturated fat ratio), grapes (resveratrol), nuts (lipids), alfalfa (chlorophyll and L-canavanine) fresh vegetable juices (nutrients easily absorbed) and Omega-3 fatty acids (flaxseed being a particularly rich plant-source). Chapter 10 lists some powerful natural anti-cancer agents that are easily found. Aged Garlic Extract, AHCC (a mushroom extract), Coenzyme Q10, Silymarin (derived from milk thistle) and pancreatic enzymes (to aid digestion and reduce side effects of chemotherapy and radiation). These are all effective in use alone or alongside other

wanting to find that diet or other therapies could make a real difference. I was willing to give an honest listen to things. Why shouldn't I be? But I wasn't *expecting* to find what I did. It's more a case of being *surprised* to find the things I was discovering. My bias was against them. I argued my way through much of what I was reading. But it's hard to argue with results, isn't it? It's hard to argue with someone who should be dead and is not. It seems more sensible to listen.

By the way, ask your doctor if traditional medicine is driven by money. It's probably the biggest frustration in most caring doctor's lives. Mary and I were saddened by how much of her traditional treatments and tests were governed by finances. It often wasn't about what was best for Mary. It was about the system, and its schedule and what it was allowed to spend.

(On a lighter note, we would chuckle over the fact that every traditional treatment we received was accompanied by steep parking fees, and every alternative treatment we eventually received wasn't. Is there a bit of irony here?)

---

therapies. The next therapies underscore the importance of the mind and spirit in fighting cancer. I'll just list the chapter titles. 11. Understand the Brain-Body Cancer Connection. 12. Cope with Stress. 13. Think Positive Thoughts. 14. Surround Yourself with Positive Friends. 15. Soul-Searching Time: Find the Will to Live. 16. Laugh all the Way to the Bank. 17. Discover the Hidden Roots of Illness (dealing with sin and forgiveness). 18. Tap Into the Power of Hope. 19. Don't Overlook Prayer Therapy. 20. Access Your Heavenly Resources.

A Survivor and a Psychologist

The final book I gave foundational attention to was a unique combination of personal and medical information. Dr. Brenda Hunter[10] is a psychologist as well as a cancer survivor. As a psychologist, she writes an especially strong segment on mending the mind— the place emotion, stress and even personality type plays in fighting cancer. Her book opened my eyes to the important roles of both stress as a fuel for cancer and hope as a weapon against cancer. After reading

---

[10] Brenda Hunter, PhD, *Staying Alive*, Colorado Springs, Colorado, Waterbrook Press, 2004. Hunter describes her own entry into the cancer zone in chapter one. Chapter 2 affirms that cancer is telling us something in our life is out of balance and we need to change it. We need to restore the body as Chapters 3-6 go on to tell us, through diet and detoxification. Brenda said farewell to salt, sugar, white flour, dairy, meat and trans fats as well as Omega-6 fatty acids found in processed foods. She said hello to organic fruit, vegetables, whole grains, legumes, soy, green superfoods, Omega 3 oils and water. Juicing is integral to nourishment. Fruit juicing to cleanse, vegetable juicing to rebuild the body. She has a good section on the 10 commandments of juicing. To detoxify, Hunter used primarily juice fasts and coffee enemas. Not only do we need to restore the body, the next section (chapters 7-14) is about mending the mind. Studies have shown that those with a fighting spirit tend to survive. Chronic stress lowers our resistance to cancer. Studies have shown a link between loneliness and cancer also. So we need our friends and other people to be close to us. Emotions and personality style are linked to cancer as well. The type C personality, typically focussed on others (who Mary was) is more prone to cancer. There is a good chapter on dealing with difficult people, stressing the importance of dealing with toxic relationships and the beauty of forgiveness. In all these areas, we must embrace life to beat cancer. The last two chapters are about healing the spirit, and talk about the important place of both faith and gratitude in conquering cancer.

it, I began doing everything I could to help Mary relax and live with hope.

We began to purposely end her day with relaxation. It would be a soothing cup of tea and a whirlpool bath by candlelight, followed by an unhurried back-rub, then our evening prayers. Partway through those prayers she was falling asleep sometimes. To me that always felt like a success. I'd simply finish our prayers myself, snuggle up to her, and peacefully fall asleep as well. The one thing I missed was hearing her say, "I love you too."

It was early summer. We were about four months into Mary's cancer walk. I was beginning to think we should try to apply some of the things we were learning. Chemotherapy alone began to feel like a prison. It seemed we had nothing to lose.

So we began to slowly change our diet. We did as many of the things we had been learning about as possible. We bought a juicer and Mary began to drink both vegetable and fruit juices. They were actually delicious. They seemed to give Mary a lot of energy. The grand-boys would often come over for a juice. There's no flavor quite like freshly juiced berries and fruit. Of course, they were not as enthusiastic about the vegetable juices. One of Mary's favorites was two carrots, an apple and two sticks of celery with a bit of cinnamon.

We began to slowly add supplements to Mary's diet as well. I wish we could have been more scientific about it, basing them on tested deficiencies in her blood chemistry. But we didn't know where to find such tests in our area. So we opted for a cautious introduction of supplements, adding a new one every few days to make sure there was no adverse reaction to them. Like I said, we had nothing to lose. We just hoped there was something to gain.

Talking to another Survivor

My nephew, Steven was on vacation and visiting his parents. He came to my work station to let me know he and his wife were praying for Mary. As we talked he mentioned that his pastor was a long-term cancer survivor. He had been diagnosed with an aggressive stage 3-4 cancer. It was so aggressive he was told he had only a few months to live. After surgery, he refused chemotherapy and radiation. He was almost too weak to function.

A few weeks later he and his wife went to a Hallelujah Acres Diet workshop. He began a strictly vegetarian diet that focused on juicing raw vegetables. Within a month he noticed an improvement in his sense of well-being. Within a couple of months - at the time he was supposed to die - he was instead getting his strength back. Twelve years later, this man is a healthy, energetic younger-than-he-should-be senior citizen, still the lead pastor of his church. He skis black diamond runs for the thrill of it, and remains cancer-free.

I called Pastor George and he graciously shared the nine principles he feels are the main reason he is alive today. Proper diet (strictly vegetarian, 85% raw, with specific vitamin supplements), ten to twelve glasses of pure water per day, daily exercise, good bowel elimination (twice daily), time in the sunshine, sleeping in fresh air, getting adequate rest, maintaining an attitude of gratitude and eliminating stress.

The Truth about Chemotherapy

Is it just me, or is it all starting to sound a bit repetitious? Why was there so much sameness to the stories of those who survive when they are not supposed to? These are just a few of the stories. There are many. Why are anti-cancer nutrition and good elimination of toxins always central to their story? And why do our doctors kept dismissing even a hint of these things?

As I was reading about the immune system, I asked our oncologist "Isn't there something we can do to boost Mary's immune system while she is on chemo?" The reply was given in a most condescending manner: "Well, obviously her immune system has not been sufficient to fight cancer, so we don't give any attention to that. It is a waste of time. We just stick to the chemotherapy." I almost felt like being condescending back. But Mary gave me the "look," so I said nothing.

It kind of puts you between a rock and a hard place when the patient is the love of your life. I increasingly felt we should be doing more than chemotherapy. The *only* option being offered by traditional medicine however was chemotherapy. I had been reading enough on traditional sites and journals of oncology to know that there are two major problems with chemotherapy.

First, chemotherapy gets harder and harder for a patient to take. The toxicity builds. Many patients have to skip treatments. There are exceptions, but for most, the side effects keep getting worse. By round seven they were painstakingly difficult for Mary. It was becoming almost intolerable. It was only her strong determination that kept her doing it. Every round was getting worse than the last at an accelerated rate. She wasn't the exception. She was the rule. That's just the way it is with chemo for most patients.

The second problem is actually more serious. Cancer adapts to chemotherapy. It develops resistance to it. The longer you are on chemotherapy, the greater the resistance tends to become. At first, tumors will shrink, or as they say "respond"[11], but round by round that will

---

[11] Do not make the mistake of thinking "response" is necessarily linked to increased survival time. In cancer, a response is defined as measureable shrinkage of 50 percent for 28 days or more. Just 28 days! So treatment can still be spoken of as a success even if in 60 days, the tumor is twice the size it was before this so called "response." In cancer research there is a lot of creative use of words, or as one writer calls it, "linguistic dodging."

diminish. The further you go, the more the resistance tends to speed up. Within a fairly short time, the newly resistant cancer will be more virulent than it was before chemotherapy started.

In a nutshell, the agony of chemo will go up while the returns go down, both on a bell curve. And for most cancer patients, it means that chemo starts out looking hopeful. Tumors shrink, measured by scans. We ourselves heard a very sincere and heartfelt, "Congratulations, your chemo is working!" But in the end it becomes its own agony, and actually makes cancer more virile.

Study after study has shown that the difference chemo makes in actual survival time for most types of cancer is measured in days or weeks at best. Do nothing, or do chemo? For a steep price in pain, the chemo may gain [12]you a few weeks of life with most solid tumor cancers. All life is precious. Life with someone you love is even more precious. Believe me when I say I know weeks are important. But, honestly, all that agony when the

---

[12] The statistics may in fact show no real advantage. Dr Ralph Moss (*Questioning Chemotherapy*, Brooklyn, N.Y., Equinox Press, 1995, pp.59-64) demonstrates 4 biases that affect the interpretation of statistics. Lead-time bias refers to the fact that most cancers are diagnosed months earlier than they used to be. The lead time is counted *with* overall survival time and makes statistics seem better than they actually may be. Stage-Migration bias (as a result of better imaging), publication bias (successful studies get more readily published, failures are shelved), and selection bias (some people's tumors are less aggressive and some people start out healthier) all mean the meager statistical gains we have made in the last 25 years may only be window dressing. It may look better statistically when nothing has actually changed.

value of it is rather unclear? They don't tell you about those bell curves or questionable statistics. Looking back, it almost seems cruel.

The four walls of chemotherapy were beginning to feel like a prison.

I was learning cancer, but would it do Mary any good?

REFLECTION

1. Where on the following list do you find yourself?

a. I believe strictly in modern traditional medicine.

b. I believe in traditional medicine but I also value alternative treatments.

c. I've given up on traditional medicine, and strictly pursue alternative and natural treatments.

2. Which position would you have put me in, at the beginning of our journey? Do you think I am still there? Why or why not?

3. Which position makes the most logical sense, and why?

4. What cautions would you give re: the use of alternatives in fighting cancer?

5. What cautions would you give someone using strictly traditional medicine to fight cancer?

6. Think again about what an anti-cancer diet looks like (low in animal fats, processed foods, sugars, salt, white flour, caffeine, alcohol, artificial sweeteners and trans fats, but high in whole grains, fruit, legumes, vegetables and clean water). What effect would such a diet have on other chronic diseases which plague our society?

      a. diabetes

      b. heart disease

      c. stroke

d. obesity

e. inflammatory diseases

f. hypertension (high blood pressure)

7. What point do you think I'm trying to make with question 6?

8. How is holding to a standard American diet less than loving to your family whether you are thinking of cancer or not?

9. Have you been to any church functions where the food has been on the wrong half of that list? Could this be wrong, even sinful?

7. The Difference Prayer Makes

One of the first things that faced us when the cancer journey started was the question of "Who are you going to tell?"

I asked Mary on the way home from the clinic after her diagnosis. First on the list, of course, was our family. Mary wanted me to do the telling that very day. But who else should we inform?

I raised it as a question, because I remember other times in our life that it really mattered to Mary "who knew." Like every time she was pregnant. The first time, I found out the hard way that there were certain people she wanted to have in the know, but others she didn't. And I found out there were certain people she wanted to tell herself. I also knew Mary tended to be a fairly private person. So we talked about it, and realized we were being pulled in two directions.

Primarily, there was the direction of privacy. Right from the beginning there was a sense that the more people knew, the more questions there would be, and the more work it would be to keep people "in the know," and the more she could possibly feel invaded. She wouldn't be known just as Mary anymore, but as "Mary Who Has Cancer."

But at the same time, we were both pulled in another direction, fueled by another concern that was immediately sensed by both of us. We felt a need for strength and wisdom and resources that were beyond ourselves. We immediately felt the need for prayer. We felt it would be good to have as many people praying for us as possible. And we knew that if we wanted people praying for us, it would really help if we shared openly with people.

We also knew that God had allowed Mary to have cancer for His own purposes. Maybe one of those purposes was to bring glory to Himself in the way we walked through it. And there wouldn't be much of that purpose being accomplished if we clung to the safety of secrecy.

So when we put it all together, we realized that the pull away from privacy was the stronger pull right from the start. Our decision was fairly quick. The discussion lasted all of five minutes. We decided that the more open we were with people, the better they'd be able to pray for us, and the more faithfully they would pray for us. And the more open we were, the more God could use this for whatever purpose He wanted. That was our strong feeling right from the start.

Does it mean we broadcast every detail, like keeping a "cancer-blog?" No, we still wanted space for Mary to just live. But we were immediately committed to erring on the side of openness rather than the side of secrecy. And this turned out to be one of the best decisions we made.

The Prayer-Loop Begins

We immediately began to try to keep people posted on what was going on. It started out as keeping people up to date by phone. Very quickly that got to be way too much. We were always on the phone. We actually got sore ears from the phone. So we began to use e-mail, sending messages out as things developed. It started out as an e-mail to family, our pastors at the church, our small group, and some close friends. I was the main writer of our e-mails, but I always discussed them with Mary before they were sent, so they were really ours.

It soon became clear that our internet connection was not up to sending mailings to more than about ten addresses at a time. The connection seemed too slow and sporadic. It would skip half the people or shut down half-way through the mailing. I lost all confidence in it, not being sure who got our e-mails and who didn't.

So we began sending a single e-mail out to one address - that of our daughter Sara - who had a better internet connection on a landline. She would forward it to an ever-growing list of e-mail addresses. With our approval, many of the people who got these e-mails began forwarding them to friends in their churches who they asked to pray for us too. And those friends would share them with other friends.   In a very short time, our e-mails were going all over the world. We were getting responses from people in different countries, even as far away as Africa. I suppose it didn't quite "go viral," (not sure if there's an exact definition of that?) but I'd at least like think it was "minor-infectious."

I sent the first e-mail in late February. Then from March 2011 to May of 2012 I sent another forty-two. A month after Mary's funeral, I sent out one more. By then people were telling me they wanted to remember the funeral, and wondered if they could have a copy of what was said. So that final e-mail was a transcript of the service celebrating Mary's life.

There were a lot of e-mails, and they were a lot of work. I labored over them. Some of them took me hours to write. I wanted to say the right thing. I wanted to be honest, even painfully so. I wanted to be more hopeful than depressed, which is hard when the news is not so hopeful. And I wanted to be sure I wasn't just speaking for me, but for Mary. Everything I wrote I would print off and have her read before it was sent out. Not once did I hit the "send" button before she had fully owned what was written. So both our hearts were laid bare in these e-mails, over and over again. We knew we had praying friends, and we felt we were doing our part to encourage them to keep on praying.

A Beautiful Thing

And so many people did pray. Family prayed. Our church prayed. Friends prayed. Fellow-patients on the cancer journey prayed. Complete strangers prayed. Like I said, the list of people who got the e-mails kept growing. What unfolded was a huge chain of prayer. It was a beautiful thing. We never planned for it to happen that way, but I don't think it was a coincidence.

I never realized the extent of the prayer chain until after Mary died. There were about five hundred people who came to be with us at two visitations on the Friday before Mary's funeral. We were blessed by the presence of many friends, family and acquaintances. But I was surprised to be blessed by others who were total strangers to me. Only, they did not talk like strangers. They talked like they had been an intimate part of our entire journey. They were part of that prayer chain. About twenty of these friends-I-had-never-met came to connect with me. They patiently waited until they had a chance to talk to me. They said stuff like, "I had to come, and I felt like I had to have a chance to talk to you. I wanted you to know I've been praying for you and Mary for the last year."

Others couldn't come, yet I received e-mails and cards from friends-I-have-never-met. The extent to which God's wonderful family surrounded Mary month after month with their prayers was truly amazing to both of us. Over a year later I am still meeting those friends.

A Plea for Prayer

To us, the purpose of the e-mails was mostly to encourage prayer. For example, let me share one of the early ones, dated March 23, 2011, about a week after Mary's surgery, when we got the pathology report from the Surgeon. This was when we first began to realize how very serious her prognosis was.

March 23, 2011

To our family and friends,

Thank you for your many prayers, cards and words of support during the early phase of this journey for Mary and I. It's taken me a while to update all of you since our meeting with the surgeon last Friday. At that meeting he showed us the pathology report. It was almost all bad news for us. (I then summarize the report. Mary's cancer had already spread to her liver, and beyond.) In his mind, the results are inevitable. He encouraged us to think in terms of quality of life, not quantity. He told us that if there were things Mary wanted to do, now was the time to do them, because the days were soon coming when she would not have the strength. Not much hope there at all!

It was all a little much for us to take in. It was very disappointing. We had hoped that his initial visual diagnoses would be tempered down, not ramped up.

So where is God in all of this? We can honestly say that He's right where He's always been, with us in all of this. We have said to each other many times that it feels as if we are being carried in this journey. That doesn't make the road easy. But it does make it a road that leads to good things for us, as He has promised in Romans 8:28. He is working for our good.

So, how do we want you to pray for us? My first inclination is to ask you to pray for healing. But I think there are probably a lot of other important things to pray for." So let me list other important things first.

1. Pray as God leads you to pray. Before you pray, ask him to show you what to pray. Get quiet before Him for a while before you pray. Then pray what He leads you to pray.

2. Pray for our attitudes to be right. Things like thankfulness, joyfulness, patience, and trusting dependence. By nature we are so much more prone to complaint, sadness, impulsive demands and worry. To come through this journey healed in body but sick in spirit is no victory at all.

3. Pray with us the third petition of the Disciple's Prayer. "Your will be done on earth as it is in Heaven." His will, whether it be healing or heaven. His will, as we interact with people. His will as we interact with each other. His will, to joyfully be our will (like Jesus, who set joy before Himself when he went to the cross, when his agonized prayer had been, "Not my will.")

4. Pray for courage. We believe we are called to fight for life. It is a gift, and diseases like cancer are against our "design." I believe cancer is an enemy. There will be temptations to fear.

5. Pray for love to flourish in our home. Between us and our children and grandchildren. Between ourselves and God. Between us and other people we meet on the cancer road.

6. Pray for our children. Pray the whole story would be one that leads them closer to God and helps them grow in Him. Pray for their reactions, their thoughts, their fears, their priorities and their faith.

7. Pray for our God-story to be real, transparent and powerful in the lives we touch. There's a bigger story here than someone having cancer. There's a story he is writing.

8. Pray for our focus. It is easy to be distracted and to let thoughts run way ahead of themselves. Pray we'd focus on today, on what is at hand. Daily work.

Daily devotions. Daily bread. Daily steps. Daily love. Daily prayer.

9. Pray for wisdom. I'm sure there will be many things we have to decide about treatments, priorities, things to ask, what to accept and what to fight. We need God's wisdom.

10. Pray for navigation. We enter the cancer clinic this Tuesday, March 29. It's a system that is probably not entirely people-friendly. Even our Doctor said people can tend to get "lost" in the process. Pray that God would guard our path, and make it straight.

11. Pray for our doctors. They know so much, but Mary's cancer is really "her" cancer, not anyone else's. Pray they'd know how to prescribe things that really are right for her.

12. Pray for her healing, if that is what would just make God look "good" to our world.

Sincerely, Mary and Bert.

You might wonder why we put so much effort into making sure people were praying for Mary and me. It's because we really believed prayer makes an actual difference.

God Is Writing Our Story

Having said all that, I don't believe prayer is simple. It is neither easy to understand or easy to do. There's more going on in prayer than just pushing the right Cosmic buttons and getting what you want. An important part of prayer is discovering and finding the strength to do what God wants.

Look again at the seventh thing I asked people to pray for. I asked them to pray for our God-story to be real, transparent and powerful in the lives we touch, because I believed there was a bigger story here than someone having cancer. God was writing a story, and cancer was part of it, whether Mary was healed or not! Prayer isn't so simple because the story isn't so simple. God doesn't give us a play-by-play on what He is doing. He actually wants it to be about faith, which really isn't faith if it is seeing or having the play-by-play.

We're pretty good at knowing what we *want* the story to be. We want health, wealth and success. We happen to be in the one percent of the world's population where we sometimes think we're being ripped off by God if our story amounts to anything less than those things. But God knows there is another story to be written. And it's the *main story*. It's the story of our lives from His *eternal perspective*. It's a story about trust, the kind of trust in God that grows through anything! As Larry Crabb puts it in his book, *Shattered Dreams*, "Life is *not* an opportunity for things to go well so we can feel good. Life *is* an opportunity for us to be forgiven for requiring God to make us feel good and for turning from Him when He doesn't. *And* life is an opportunity to live through shattered dreams and discover that we really long to abandon ourselves to the Perfect Love of God, the love he revealed when Jesus died. It is an opportunity to trust Him..." [13]

That, I think, is why prayer can be such a struggle. We struggle with what we don't know about the story he is writing in us. And we struggle with what we do know about the story he is writing in us. Our will so often looks better to us than His. So I struggled, and still struggle with that aspect of prayer. It isn't so simple.

I Was Sure God Would Heal Her

So what do I do when God doesn't answer my most impassioned prayer? Because that's what happened. In spite of what the doctors predicted, I had been asking God to heal Mary. And God seemed to keep encouraging that kind of prayer.

Please don't be among those who pass judgment on me by concluding that maybe there was something "deficient" in my prayers. That is a

---

[13] Larry Crabb, Shattered Dreams, Colorado Springs, Colorado, Waterbrook Press, 2001, p.45, emphasis Crabb's)

shallow conclusion which some too easily leap to. Please don't go there. My prayers were truly prayers of faith. I did not just "work it up." I truly believed God was going to heal Mary. Honestly, I did. As I shared in one of the e-mails, the night of September 2, 2011 I had a vivid dream that Mary and I were looking at the results of a C.T. Scan that showed all of her tumors completely removed! They were all gone! It was an incredibly vivid dream, unlike any dream I had ever experienced.

Just 28 days later, it was Mary's last birthday, September 30, 2011. On Friday evening, Mary's whole family came to our house to celebrate her life. We enjoyed a delicious supper together, and Mary was surrounded by love. She felt like she wanted to say something to everyone there. So she had written out a speech, in which she thanked each of her family members for their love and prayers. She closed by quoting our wedding verses from The Message Bible. It says, "Trust God from the bottom of your heart; don't try and figure out everything on your own. Listen for God's voice in everything you do. Everywhere you go, he's the one who will keep you on track." (Proverbs 3:5-6).

It was one of the very few times I ever saw Mary make a speech. Speeches just were not her thing. But she was determined to make one that night! And she did it well! You could have heard a pin drop. I was sitting next to her, holding her hand, and I was so proud of her. It was just one more time I saw her step out of her comfort zone to do what she simply felt she should. Those were beautiful moments.

When she was done, I talked to everyone for a while. I thanked them for their love and support. And I thanked them for their many prayers. I didn't write out what I was going to say, I just shared what was on my heart at the moment. And I distinctly remember that I talked to our family about healing. That vivid dream was still playing in my mind. I told them that even though statistics say almost no one with Mary's advanced stage of bowel cancer beats it, I was sure that somehow Mary would. She would be that one-in-a-hundred person. I was sure of it, and I said so.

And God seemed to be the one convincing me of it. It wasn't just the dream. Over and over He seemed to encourage me to believe big! I remember telling Mary a few days earlier that I had been reading a scripture that encourages us to ask big. So I responded with what I thought was a big, big request: "Lord, I pray You would give Mary and I ten more good years together." Then something in me thought, "Why not bigger?" So I asked Him, for twenty years, then the thought came again, so I asked God to give us thirty more years together. I prayed that many times in the days surrounding her birthday. I prayed it with full confidence. I had no doubt at all that God could heal her, and I was sure He would! I felt that He was the One encouraging me to pray for those thirty years.

But What if He Did Not?

But God didn't give us what we were all asking. God did not give me what I was sure He was going to. Instead, near midnight on May 30, my dream was shattered. Can you feel with me the agony of that? Can you see how it could make prayer so much more difficult? So what am I supposed to do when my prayer isn't answered the way I expected it to be?

It didn't take very long to realize I had some very definite choices. I could choose to escape the pressure of this shattered dream, my new reality. If this is life, and not even prayer works right, then how can I just escape this pain? Lots of people choose escape at this point in life. They do it by _____. You could fill in the blank, couldn't you? You know about the great escapes, ranging from addictions to withdrawal, to the ultimate withdrawal - suicide.

In fact, the choice to "escape" is one of the few things that had Mary a little worried about me. Just a few days before she died, our daughter Jenn (Nate's wife) was talking to Mary. "Mom, are you worried about Dad?" Jenn asked. Mary knew me as only a life-long lover could. She thought for a moment then replied, "No, Jenn. He'll be okay... but just don't let him become a hermit." She knew the form of escape that would be most tempting for me.

So, for the record, partly armed by her words, let me say that I don't aim intentionally or unintentionally to be part of any such escapism. I know that path would only take me from a shattered dream to an even more shattered life. That's what escapism actually does to a person, isn't it? It just shatters what's left.

A Subtle Form of Denial

The thought came to me that Christians can sometimes practice a subtle form of denial here. When a deep prayer is not answered, and a dream is shattered, we can misuse words in a way that is actually a kind of denial. Let me try to illustrate that.

I was once asked to come and be part of a prayer meeting for a man who was in the final stages of cancer. Two of us who were pastors were asked to come. I prayed first, asking God to watch over my brother, to make His love and grace very evident in this circumstance, to give strength to the entire family, and to take my brother home gently if that was His plan. I also prayed, confessing that I believed God still had the power to heal my brother if he chose to do so, and asked for that healing in Jesus' powerful Name. Then the other pastor prayed. His prayer was entirely about healing. There was no other request. He went on for quite a while praying for that request. And he was very insistent in his request. "Heal, God, Heal!" Those were his exact words, spoken many times. I'm sure he didn't intend it that way, but he used the word so many times it almost sounded to me like he was commanding God to "heel!"

I was struck by the contrast in our prayers. I was actually a little annoyed by the way he talked to God. I thought to myself, "Heel!" is a command you give to your dog, not to God. At the same time, it also made me wonder if I was "fudging" my prayers a bit, not having faith to ask as boldly and consistently as my praying friend did. It got me thinking.

A few days later, sadly, the man we were praying for was dead. I went to the same home to pray with the family and the same praying friend was there. And we both prayed again, only this time we were praying for the grieving family. I can remember again being confused and a little annoyed by the way my praying friend was now praying.

What confused me was that his prayer was still about healing. Only this time, he was actually thanking God for answering the prayer we had prayed a few days before. "Thank You God, for answering our prayers and totally healing our brother." I couldn't help it. That annoyed me. "But wait," I thought to myself, "He's dead! Our prayers were *not* answered were they?"

It seemed like my praying friend was toying with the meaning of words. It seemed somehow less than honest to me.   Like a denial of the obvious. It's like he couldn't bring himself to say, "We're disappointed, Lord God, that You did *not* answer our prayers (I'm not sure why that should be so hard to say. If God is God, that should totally be His prerogative, should it not?)."

Instead of thanking God for healing, when He didn't heal, why not be honest? Why not pray, "God, you didn't answer our prayers for healing. You allowed that dream to shatter! But we do not believe it is because You couldn't make the dream come true, or because You do not care about us or about the dream. Instead, it is because You see a bigger dream! You are more concerned about writing a bigger story in and through our departed brother's life. It is such a story of praise now! And you are also more interested in writing another story in the lives of those of us who are left behind (back to what Crabb says?). Help us know that story more deeply. Please give us the strength to face this shattered dream and go on living Your story." Doesn't that prayer feel more real?

Another Hard Question

This leads me to another hard question. It's a very painful question, one that has me a bit confused. It's one of those "Why" questions. I sometimes ask myself why God would allow me (even lead me) to think healing was going to be part of the story He was writing? Why let me think so when He knew all along it was not actually the story He was writing? That is not an easy question is it? I don't think I'm the only one puzzled by it.

Here's what I am tentatively concluding. In my humble opinion, and it is a very humble opinion on this point, I'm starting to believe this too was part of His loving mercy to me. You say, "How could leading someone to believe a delusion like that be mercy in any form?" Here's why I think it probably is a mercy. I asked myself this question. "What would life have been like for me this last year if I did *not* have the confidence I had?" "What would life have been like if I did *not* believe God not only could but would heal Mary?"

When I ask myself that question, I suddenly realize something. Believing what I confidently did was so freeing! It was such a beautiful way to "live" with Mary's cancer. It took a lot of the pressure off me, and gave me such hope! My day to day wasn't filled with worry about Mary dying, and how she would handle it, and how I could ever possibly handle it? Instead, I was thinking about her living, and what I could do to help her live. I was free to just concentrate on loving her and walking with her!

A Severe Mercy

The idea that our confidence in healing was actually a mercy is probably true of Mary as well as me. Mary was never very fond of farewells. I got to know that side of her when we moved up to North

Ontario. Her parents or one of her sisters would come to visit us for a week. She'd look forward to that for at least a month, anticipating it more and more as the time approached. And we'd have an absolutely great visit, no matter who came. But then I would notice Mary going a little quiet, and some of the fun of the visit being lost at about halfway through. On day four I'd catch a hint or two of sadness, by day five it was visible, by day six it was completely noticeable, and by the last night of the visit her mood would be undeniably sad. I knew why. I knew she was thinking of having to say goodbye. Goodbyes always made her sad.

"I'll See You Later"

That part of who Mary was became noticeable to me again in the last two weeks of her life. After that wonderful celebration of Mom's eighty-third birthday Mary and I were at home the next evening. John and Kathy (Mary's sister and her husband) had to fly back to Texas the next morning. On their way to the airport, they had planned to stop in and say good bye to Mary. We all knew it might be the very last good bye they had. It was so hard. We knew it was time for them to say it. They had to go, but they didn't want to leave.

Mary was lying on the couch. Kathy was leaning on her in a long and tearful embrace. We were all struggling, knowing what we had to say and just not wanting to do it. John was pacing, visibly upset, clenching his fists, pain etched in his face. Suddenly he burst out, in his very Texan accent, "Maaan, this just SUUUCKS!" I agreed that it did. Then Kathy sobbed, "Oh Mary, I just don't want to say goodbye. I can't say goodbye to you! I just can't!"

Her words hung on the air for a minute. We were all crying except Mary. Mary looked her in the eye and replied in a quiet and steady voice. "Then don't say goodbye, Kathy. Just say, "See you later, because you will, no matter what." So that's what Kathy said, and it became what Mary started to say to everyone. For all of us, it was never goodbye anymore after that. It was always, "I'll see you later."

It was part of who Mary was. She disliked goodbyes. So maybe for her too, the belief that she was going to be healed was a "mercy" from God. It spared her the agony of a long, long goodbye.

These have been some "heavy" thoughts on prayer haven't they? They have been a little more theology than story. I hope I've kept you "with" me enough so that I can ask you a couple of rather personal questions about your praying. I ask them because I believe that without balance in this area, our prayers can too easily become useless religious exercises instead of the incredible blessing they were for Mary and me through this cancer collision.

REFLECTION

1. For you, is prayer too simple? What I mean is, for you, is prayer all about *your* story (i.e. about getting what YOU want)?

2. For you, does prayer include opening yourself to the story God may want to write in your life? If so, how are you doing that?

3. I ask this gently, but for you, is asking God to "HEEL" (or submit to you) part of your praying?

4. To follow up, if your honest answer to the last question was yes, what are the possible negative repercussions? What positive repercussions do you think there might be?

5. Galatians 6:2 says, "Carry each other's burdens, and in this way you will fulfill the law of Christ." How does this command impact the question of "Who are you going to tell?" when it comes to cancer?

6. My tentative conclusion is that God let me believe Mary was going to be healed, and that it was a display of His mercy toward me. Why would you agree or disagree with this conclusion?

7. That minor-infectious prayer-chain was one of the biggest blessings to come to Mary and me in the cancer journey. How can we improve on our prayer-chains among Christians, so that more people are blessed this way?

8. Our Walk through Therapy

The whole rhythm of Mary's life began to revolve around chemotherapy. Every other Wednesday was chemo day. The day before, we'd have to go to town, get her blood-work done, meet with the oncologist to be weighed and have her white cell count checked so they could compute her maximum tolerated dose of chemo. Between travel, waiting, drawing blood, waiting again, then having the actual appointment, and travelling home again, it would chew up three to four hours of the day.

Chemo days we'd go for a good strong walk in the morning, Mary would take her anti-nausea pills and put the numbing cream on her Port-a-Cath. Mary had gone for day-surgery before her first chemo to install a catheter from her jugular vein to a "port" inserted under her skin just above her right breast. Though it was painful for a few days, it actually was worth it. Her veins never could have stood up to the chemo she received, and later, the catheter would become used for alternative treatments many times.

We would motor down for treatment, about a forty-five minute drive. After the first few rounds, we were able to avoid the parking fees. A Christian family owned a house near the hospital, and welcomed cancer patients to use their driveway for free parking while undergoing treatments, a small mercy.

We'd walk in through the north entrance and wind our way to the Cancer Centre. After swiping her card we'd usually wait up to half an hour for Mary to be called in. She'd get seated in her delegated reclining chair, have her stats checked and rechecked, and then the nurse assigned to her would go and get Mary's basket of drugs.

The chemo drugs are so toxic that the nurse would be completely gowned in latex in case a drop of chemo spilled on her. [14]

The nurse would start Mary's Port-a-Cath. This involved piercing through Mary's skin and into its pad section with a hooked needle, then attaching tubings to I.V. bottles on the stand. Some nurses were good at starting the catheter, and others, not so much. I was surprised at the difference. Mary got to know who was good and who wasn't. I'd usually get a little groan or a smile depending on who was coming to work our recliner.

Once the I.V. was inserted and primed, the nurse would start Mary's first bag of drugs. Mary would be reasonably comfortable for an hour. We'd chat and read magazines. Then, with the next bag of chemo, nausea would set in. It was usually quite

---

[14] I was surprised by how toxic. It is so toxic that the Cancer Centre gives out free condoms so that the patient's spouse can be protected from the tiny bit of chemo they could contact through intercourse. I was actually warned that if I had unprotected sex with Mary during the first three days of chemo, I placed myself in danger of developing cancer. The same drugs that kill cancer can give you cancer? Go figure!

sudden. Mary would be comfortable one moment, and then with a lurch, the battle would be on. I could always tell. In an instant, her face would turn pale, and she would clench her jaws. Visiting hours would be over. Now it was nursing time.

By the third bag of chemo, Mary would be losing all her energy. She would visibly deteriorate before my eyes. She would start to tremble. I'd have to pile on a heated blanket and a quilt even though it was so warm in there that I'd be wearing a short-sleeved shirt. She wouldn't be able to read her magazine at all anymore. Her eyes lost their focus and their life, taking on a hazy grey tone instead of their normal baby blue. It almost looked like her body was going into shock.

The whole process would usually take about three to four hours, depending on how well the catheter had been inserted. The last bag of chemo was always smaller and faster than the others. After the first time, Mary began to dread that final bag. Though taken through her I.V., the chemo would instantly make Mary's tongue go fuzzy, giving it an overpowering "tinny" taste. She would chew on ice cubes to try to diminish the side effect, but her mouth would taste like a factory for days.

Then they'd attach the portable bag of chemo. It was to be placed in a take-home pouch (you guessed it, we had to supply the pouch), with a pressurized vessel that would administer the last drug in a non-stop fashion for the next forty-eight hours. We were issued a bio-hazardous material spill kit that we had to carry in the car in case the connecting tubing got detached and the chemo somehow spilled.

By the time we left the hospital, it would be about four hours from when we entered, and Mary would be completely exhausted. I'd drive her home as directly and gently as I could. I tried not to weave in traffic too much or hit any bumps. She would be cold and sweating at the same time, kind of huddled in her seat, trying gamely to fight off nausea.

She just wanted to get home, so she could lie down. I would get her comfortable, and she'd try to take a nap. The rest of the afternoon would be spent attempting to rest, and to consume a few calories of nourishment. Very little food ever made it down.

The first evening Mary would normally not be up to much of a walk. At best it was a few hundred feet. We really didn't call it a walk. It was just getting some air. But she would always want to do that. It made her feel a bit better.

Admiring her Every Step

Days two and three of chemo were worse than the first. The forty-eight-hour slow-drip of continuous chemo was very uncomfortable. It contained a corticosteroid to help her body deal with the effects of the main drugs. The steroid made it almost impossible for her to sleep more than brief periods at a time. That led to utter exhaustion. But even then, she would still want to try walking. My admiration for her grew with each step she took. She was not an "in your face" kind of person, but beneath her quietness she had a strength. She was walking because of determination and desire more than anything else.

On those days we didn't make it to the Crown Land. It was just up and down the top half of our street. Our driveway was rather long and all uphill. It would take three to four stops for us to get her to the top. She would never complain, or ask us to stop. That took too much energy. I just knew by the pressure of her hand that it was time to breathe for a few moments. She would lean against me for a while then whisper "okay" and we'd do another quarter of the driveway.

Friday noon was usually her de-access. One of our friends, Lois, took on the de-access trip as her personal ministry to Mary. It became her thing.

Usually on de-access Fridays, Lois would come to our house, pick Mary up, go with her to the Cancer Centre, through de-access (never quite getting the nerve to actually look when the needle was being pulled), then drive her home, fix a light lunch and visit with her for a while. De-access would bring almost immediate relief, but it would still be a slow day for Mary. By Saturday she would start to regain a little bit of energy. Her eyes would begin to shine. The walks would be at half speed, but getting a little longer. By Sunday afternoon, she'd feel able to do the hill, and we'd make it to the Crown Land, her favorite place to walk. She would feel stronger, ever so slowly, each day.

This was the pattern, April through June. By then we were noticing a shift. It was taking Mary longer every time to regain her strength. And the nausea was staying longer.

Looking for More

I was becoming convinced that Mary should be doing other therapies as an addition to chemotherapy. As July came, we began to search for alternative therapies in our area. By the last week of July we found a clinic in Toronto that offered a number of them.

We went for our first treatment there on the Tuesday of her off-chemo week. Mary received an I.V. treatment of high-dose vitamin C accompanied by other vitamins and trace minerals. She had also been increasing her intake of other vitamins, probiotics and juices.

Until that Tuesday morning, round eight of chemotherapy had been going very poorly. It was already six days since it had been administered, but Mary remained so weak, lacking in energy. She was fragile. Everything hurt. On the way home from the Vitamin C therapy, however, she was like a new woman. Some of her bounce was back. And it lasted for days. A week later, going into round nine of chemotherapy, she still had more energy. And she actually had less severe side effects going out of that round. It made a strong impression on me.

The next week we had been given the gift of staying at a cottage on Twin Sisters Lakes, near Marmora, Ontario, a three-hour drive from the alternative clinic (barring traffic problems). We came to the cottage Monday morning and hit the sack early that night. We got up at 4:00 a.m. the next morning so we could be at the alternative clinic for the 7:00 a.m. opening, to get Mary another Vitamin C treatment. The last one had helped her so much it was worth the six hours of driving.

Pulled Two Ways

So we entered a new phase. It was chemo as usual, on Tuesday and Wednesday of week one.

Then, on Tuesday of week two, first thing in the morning, we'd drive to the big city, and she'd get either a high dose vitamin C treatment, or Hydrogen Peroxide. The C would give her a huge boost in energy. By Tuesday evening her walk would definitely be picking up again. On the C weeks, we'd get two to three extra days of good walking. Even on the Peroxide weeks, by the weekend, we'd be doing her favorite trails again. We'd have about three days of what she would call a "good walk." A good walk meant at least an hour, and at a good pace. Then it would be chemo Wednesday again, and she'd be knocked back down again.

That became our rhythm through the late summer of 2011. It was like her body was being pulled in two directions. She was being pulled down by chemo, and pulled up by her alternative treatments and by her incredible will. Treatments and Scans and round after round of chemo piled up on her body. Five, then ten, then twelve rounds. We counted off fourteen rounds of chemo. I don't think she could have gotten that far without the alternative treatments giving her a boost.

By round twelve, every part of her body was aching for most of the two weeks. Her feet hurt, her legs hurt, her back hurt, her stomach was usually upset and her arms and shoulders ached. Even her eyes were actually hurting. Her vision was noticeably impaired. We began to suspect that the chemo was killing her more than the cancer was.

We asked our cancer specialist which of the pains she was feeling could be the result of chemo. We discovered that all of them could.

Meanwhile, the tests were now showing no perceptible shrinkage in tumors. It seemed we were nearing the end of the effective shelf-life of her chemotherapy.

Her bones began to just ache. They did a bone scan to see if cancer had gone there. That turned out to be a negative, so Mary concluded that what she was feeling was the result of chemo killing her bone cells. Her body was almost screaming at her to just stop! So on round thirteen, she asked for an extra week off from chemo, and for a lower dose to be given to her. The extra week seemed to help her a bit, and round thirteen at a lower dose didn't hit her quite as hard. But it was still so hard.

Listening to Her Body

We began to talk more about what Mary's body was telling her. She was getting a stronger and stronger sense that chemo was hurting more than it was helping by now. She endured one more round, round fourteen, in November 2012. Then she told me tearfully she just couldn't do chemo anymore.

We were booked for round fifteen, and decided we'd tell the doctor she didn't want to do any chemo at all anymore. We had been doing a lot of talking. I had been reading about Metronomic Low Dose Chemotherapy. Studies had shown it to have positive affect against cancer but without the powerful side effects. We wanted to try that instead of what we were now doing.

It turned out to be a very negative doctor's appointment. He dismissed Metronomic Therapy outright, without any discussion at all. He said Mary wasn't "approved" for the funding to do that. She was approved for the "standard care" she was getting now. I asked why she couldn't just get approved, especially since it would be much cheaper. But he dismissed that too. Didn't even want to talk about it.

Because I did the talking, and we were not just meekly agreeing with his desires, the doctor actually became rather angry with me.

I don't want to judge him too harshly. I think he was sincerely focused on extending life. I tell myself he was doing the only thing he knew. I did wonder if he was more concerned with his statistics than with Mary. I do know he quit responding to me, and talked only to Mary. He actually turned his back on me, and focused only on her. And somehow he managed to talk her out of what had been her decision. Somehow he talked her into agreeing to at least a couple more rounds, reduced by a third of the strength, and before we knew it, our four minutes were up, he left the room smiling, and we were booked to come back tomorrow to continue chemo.

We left the Centre and got back to the car. I was puzzled. This isn't where I had thought Mary wanted to go. I found myself wondering if maybe the Doctor was seeing something I wasn't.

So I purposely raised the subject with Mary in a way that put it all in her court. She was quiet, deep in thought. I knew her. I could tell she was tense about something, very upset. So I asked her, "How are *you* with this, Mary? Are *you* okay with coming in tomorrow? Because if you are happy with it, I just want you to know I'm 100 percent behind you. I'll be with you every step of the way."

She immediately responded with fire in her eyes, "No, I'm *not* happy. I'm not sure how that happened. One minute we were done with chemo, and I felt so relieved. Now I'm going back, and I feel all burdened down again. How did that happen?" She began to quietly weep.

I wanted her to clarify. I lifted her chin, and our eyes connected. I had to hear it straight from her heart. "Are you saying you definitely don't want to go back tomorrow? Are you for sure, for sure?"

Through tears she said she did not want to go back. So I told her with finality, "Then we won't! I'll call the doctor's office as soon as we get home and tell him. That's how we'll do it. And he won't change my mind, I promise you that. And listen, any time you change your mind, we can go back to it. Are you good with that?" The look on her face was one of utter relief. Like any other major decision we've ever made, it was sealed with a kiss.

I phoned the doctor's office, and stuck to my guns on Mary's decision. And I'm convinced the decision was right. The next few weeks were weeks of healing for Mary. She kept doing the alternative treatments, now going every week. Without the chemo to knock her down, she actually improved dramatically. Her disease never improved, but she did. After just a few weeks off chemo, her bones felt better again, and the walks became faster and longer. We were moving into the five best months of our life together.

How could I say they were the best when her cancer wasn't cured, in fact, was still advancing? I say it because without the chemo knocking her down, she could so much better live those months to the full. That is exactly what we did. Lots of love and laughter and conversation. Just enjoying every second of our life together. That was us after chemo.

A New Pattern

All through December and into the New Year and up to spring of 2012 the pattern changed for us. Now it was trips to the city every week for alternative treatments. Intravenous Vitamin C and Peroxide at one clinic, Insulin Potentiated Low Dose Chemotherapy, and Low Dose Metronomic Chemotherapy at another. The low doses bothered her stomach a bit, but they never knocked her flat. She even sipped tea and ate her packed lunch as she was being treated at the alternative clinics. It was always visiting hours there.

She was stronger than she had been in months. The winter was so mild that many of our walks were taken on the Crown Land. As spring came, we wandered our favorite trails almost every day. The walks were long and they were relaxed. Often we talked, but a lot of our communication was not verbal. We only let go of each other's hand where the trail skirted a puddle. Then we'd link up again. We'd get to the lake and pause for a while, gazing out over the water toward the north shore of Lake Scugog. The moment blessed with another kiss, we'd usually take a different trail home. There were lots of spontaneous kiss-breaks on those walks. All she'd have to do was stop walking, and send me her "kiss-me" look.

Easter Sunday, 2012, was an unusually nice day for the second week of April. We had done the first half of our walk, and finished our habitual pause by the Lake, complete with a kiss. As we turned to go, Mary pointed out a trail that headed further West. We'd never done it before, and she wondered what was around the bend. It was a beautiful day and the trail seemed to call to us, so we decided to take it as far as she felt able. Up past a pond and a swampy area, we discovered a quiet meadow. We were the only people there.

We wandered up an old farmer's trail, as the sun was shining and a gentle breeze was blowing. Near a tall pine the grass felt dry enough to sit on. We lay down and gazed up at the sky. I lay on my back with my jacket as a pillow. My legs were spread enough for Mary to lie on her back between them, with her head and her shoulders on my torso. I was her pillow. It was so comfortable. A few wispy clouds idled by. Time stood still for us as we relaxed there. We communicated deeply in that hour. Occasionally, we used words. Mostly she lay there as I gently caressed her hair and face and neck.

We both noticed at the same time that a large hawk seemed to be checking us out. I think to the bird we may have seemed like carrion, we were so still. The fowl was about seventy feet above us hovering, barely moving its wings, playing with the breeze as it slowly circled seeming to fix its gaze on us. We could see beneath its wings, and were surprised at how many colors were there and how large and graceful it was. It was so quiet all we could hear was our own breathing and the soft whispers of a breeze.

The gentle solitude of those moments was incredible. It was just me and Mary and God (by His Spirit and creation). Gratitude, peace, love and time. Time to just be *with* one another. It felt almost sacred.

Some Chemo Thoughts

Am I saying I'm sorry Mary took as much chemo she did? Yes, I think I am. Looking back, I think it did Mary more harm than good. Did it extend her life? Possibly, but at much too high a cost in pain. The initial shrinkage it brought to tumors never lasted very long at all. It actually robbed her of quality-life more than it extended chronological-life.

After being intimately part of Mary's walk through chemo, I've reached some personal conclusions. If I found out tomorrow that I had cancer, stage four, would I take chemo? I would not, unless I had one of those specific cancers that have a high rate of effective response[15] (that is

---

[15] Chemotherapy has been clearly demonstrated as effective in certain types of cancer, irrespective of stage.

remission or significant life extension, not just shrinkage of tumors for 28 days) to chemo.

If I did take chemotherapy, I would first seek out chemo-sensitivity testing (available through private clinics, and probably worth what it will cost) of my cancer cells to make sure the chemo I was taking was the absolutely "right" one for me. That would increase the chance of chemo doing what I hoped.

I would be much more inclined to take chemo if the doctors were fairly hopeful that no more than five or six rounds of it would shrink my tumors enough to allow surgery. Surgery, though accompanied by pain and risks, is a hugely beneficial way to reduce the cancer load on a person's body! I would certainly not take

---

From what I have read, it is truly effective in treating Acute Lymphatic Leukemia, Hodgkin's Disease, Testicular Cancer, and some rare forms of cancer(Choriocarcinoma, Wilm's Tumor, and Retinoblastoma). If there are others, I am not aware of them, but am certainly open to correction. Chemotherapy also offers about a six-month extension of life in Small Cell Lung Cancer patients, and about eighteen months in Stage 3 Ovarian Cancer patients. As far as I know, what I have just written is documented fact. For a reasoned discussion of that, see Dr. Ralph Moss, *Questioning Chemotherapy*, Brooklyn, New York, Equinox Press, 1995. Unfortunately, Mary's cancer was not in that small list of cancers. Instead it was in the majority of cancers, the ones that are not truly helped by chemotherapy except in early stages.

chemotherapy or submit to surgery without first having an adequate chemotherapy-support and surgical support program[16] in place.

I would adhere to a strong anti-cancer diet. I don't think it is ever too late for that. Nor is it ever too early. I would live as full a life as I could. Full of love, full of worship, full of things that give me energy, full of connectedness to those I love, consciously blessing the next generation. What's the point of fighting for life if your life is not worth living? I would not allow cancer to take over my life. I know from walking with Mary how much strength comes from fullness of living. I also know how much strength can be needed.

As much as I could, I would pursue the alternative therapies that seemed to help Mary's energy so much, like Vitamin C. I would also try to get into a clinic that did Hyperthermia (heat therapy) which is gaining recognition all over the

---

[16] See Dr. Keith Blocks, *Life Over Cancer*, New York, N.Y., Bantam/Dell, 2009. Block has written an exceptional book based on decades of treating cancer patients. A proper support program consists first of lifestyle changes. A good (plant-based) diet, fitness (aerobic, flexibility, and strength), stress-reduction and proper rest are essential right from the start of treatments. Your own biochemical environment must be addressed so that it has adequate oxidization, good anti-inflammatory levels and a strengthened immune system. Surgery, chemotherapy and radiation all should have effective support programs that minimize side effects while maximizing their effectiveness against cancer cells. I read Dr. Block's book after Mary died. I wish I had read it before she was diagnosed. The information would have shaped our cancer battle much differently. It would have changed how we approached both surgery and chemotherapy. I think it would have given Mary her best fighting chance. I highly recommend this book.

world, especially Holland and Germany, but just starting to be available in Canada, though not funded by our medical system. I regret that we didn't learn about that therapy until the last month or two of Mary's life. I think it would have helped her.

Finally, I would take a crash course on the particular cancer I was diagnosed with before I did any treatment at all (unless an emergency situation like a blocked bowel or internal bleeding required it). I would ask my doctor, "Is this an emergency, or will a one to three week time-out before I do anything be okay?" The crash course I recommend should only take that long.

For the crash course, I would contact Dr. Ralph Moss, who is the director of Cancer Communications Inc, of Lemont, Pennsylvania. He has studied and written books and articles about cancer since 1980. Through cancerdecision.com (or phone, 1-800-980-1234) he offers well documented and carefully studied educational material on cancer causes and treatments. He has written a report specific to most cancers. He is widely quoted, but to get the most out of his years of study, it's important to get the actual report. That is the only way to read what he is saying in its proper context.

I found out about his services and purchased his Moss Report on Colorectal Cancer (the best $300 I spent in the cancer journey) about four months before Mary died. I wish I had purchased it sooner, because even then it was a big help in deciding what alternative treatments to pursue and which to avoid.

I would also read Dr. Keith Block's, *Life Over Cancer* (see footnote above). It is not light reading, but to date, it is the best all-round book I've read on cancer. I would follow the plan outlined in this book as much as I could. It is comprehensive, and aims to work with both you and your medical team against cancer.

I am speaking very personally here. This is what I think "I" would do. What you think you should do may not be the same as what I think.

But back to Mary, and our story. Was a diet change worth it for Mary? Were alternative treatments worth it? She died. In fact, she barely outlived her original prognosis. Did the treatments do anything for her?

I think they did. Up until the last weeks she had amazing levels of strength. Until she got pneumonia about a month before she died, we still went on long walks almost every day. The results of the final medical test she had were very negative. Her liver was almost overrun with cancer, it was back in her bowels and it was all through her abdomen. We asked, and the surgeon concluded Mary only had a few days, at the most two weeks to live. Our doctor agreed. She said, "When I look at the test results, I agree, but when I look at you (Mary) I disagree. You look so much better than you should."

A few days later she couldn't hold down good food anymore. All she could consume was jello and ginger ale. She couldn't take further alternative treatments. The change in her was almost immediate. Within a day, that appearance of being "better than she should" was gone. Suddenly Mary looked as sick as she was. It was striking!

The treatments seemed to make a difference in the area of pain as well. Colon Cancer can be very painful in the later stages. Based on her scans, our doctor was expecting things to be painful for Mary. She educated us on the importance of "conditioning" Mary's pain receptors to be properly responsive to morphine. She said things like, "Believe me, you'll need this!" We had Mary hooked up to an electronically controlled morphine dispenser at home. Mary dutifully tried it for a day, but it made her very groggy, and she knew she just didn't need it. So she cut the dose to twenty-five percent or less of what the doctor had suggested.

Thankfully, the need for pain medication never really went up much from that. Mary just didn't have the pain she should have. It was that way right to the end. Even in the hospital during her last day of life, the most the drip was ever turned up to was "2" out of "10." The doctor was on the alert for signs of pain, sure she'd need much more morphine, but it just never happened. I'll always be thankful for that. It would have hurt me so much more to see her in agony. But it wasn't about pain in that hospital room. As I'll share later, it was more about peace.

I've been talking to you about some very hurtful things brought on by cancer. But we found our cancer walk did some positive things for us as well, even when the walk got very hard.

It continued to sharpen our love. Both the love between Mary and I, and the love between us and our children, grandchildren and extended family was given an upward boost through cancer. The harder the cancer hit her, the deeper our love grew. The love between us and God's people grew by leaps and bounds. It wasn't just a cancer journey, it was a love journey.

The harder the walk became, the more our words were refined. We were already in the habit of saying good words, but that was made even stronger. We said so many truly important things to each other. It's not that we sat around trying to think of important things to say. We just didn't leave things unsaid anymore. Our home was verbally blessed because of cancer. I think of a simple conversation between Mary and me. It happened on one of those busy days near the end, a day full of treatments and tiredness, and lots of just "caring" for Mary. As I was bringing her something to eat--between a load of laundry and cleaning up, and looking after medications--I think a bit of weariness was showing on my face.

I suddenly caught her looking at me. It was one of those "Something is on my mind" looks. I immediately stopped what I was doing to connect with her. Her eyes filled with tears, and she said,

"I'm just so sorry, hon." "Sorry for what?" I asked. "I'm sorry that I've become a burden to you," she said. I didn't have to think long about that one. "Oh, Mary! *You're* not a burden to me. You will never be a burden to me. Your cancer is a burden. But not you. Mary, you are anything but a burden to me. You are the biggest blessing in my life."

It wasn't a long conversation, but it immediately reached soul level. And it was like that with a lot of our conversations. They were deeper and more connected than ever before. Even the silences were deeper. We had become "us" like never before.

Cancer taught us to live in the moment. It taught us not to worry about stuff we had spent most of our lives worrying about. It made us more worry-free than we had ever been, especially Mary.

Was there pain? Yes, but it was never unbearable. Was there sorrow and hurt? More than you can imagine. But did the negatives have the final word on Mary's cancer? Not even close!

Splash-Overs from Heaven

On October 27, almost five months after Mary died, our daughter Aimee sent me an e-mail from Halifax. She had read that Joni Eareckson Tada was fighting breast cancer. Joni had tweeted an update the day before and Aimee forwarded it to me. The update went back and forth between comments by a correspondent, Kim Lawton, and Joni. I was amazed and blessed again by this dear sister's courage and faith. It's been her life's story. In particular I was taken by part of the article, where Lawton talks with Joni about chemo. She writes, "More daunting was chemotherapy....the chemo took a severe toll on her body. She says it was in those dark moments that she saw the power of her faith."

Then the article quotes Tada. "I remember one time my husband was driving me home from chemotherapy and I was particularly nauseous, and we started talking about how our sufferings, this cancer is like a little splash-over from hell, that kind of wakes you up out of your spiritual slumber like "Whoa!" And so, then we started thinking, well then, what are splash-overs of heaven? Are they those days when everything is easy and breezy and bright, and there are no problems? He looked at me in the rearview mirror and said, "No, I think splash-overs from heaven are finding God, or finding Jesus in your splash-overs from hell." (http://www.pbs.org/wnet/religionandethics/epis odes/october-26-2012)

Even in the worst parts of our walk through therapy, we were enriched by those splash-overs from heaven. For those I will always be grateful.

REFLECTION

About Chemotherapy

1. What do you know about the effectiveness of chemotherapy when it comes to specific types of cancer? Why would it be better to learn this sooner rather than later?

2. What approach does your family doctor take in fighting cancer? What part does chemotherapy play in that approach? Why would it be worth talking to him or her about it?

3. What possible risks are involved in talking to your doctor? Are those risks worth it?

4. What might the benefits be? Do the benefits outweigh the risks?

5. What alternative therapies are available in your area? Would it be worth doing some research on them now? Which ones would you be willing to pay the price for (because pay you will at this point in Canadian medical history)?

6. How much money are you saving to an emergency fund? If someone in your family gets cancer (chances are about one in three), why could you possibly need such a fund?

About Love

1. How do you make decisions in your household regarding treatments of illnesses, like cancer? What does this question have to do with love?

2. How do you react to Joni's "splash-over from heaven" talk? Is it just some kind of religious jargon? How is it real?

3. If it is real, when is the best time to find your own personal connection to Jesus, or to improve your connectedness to Him?

4. Which statement do you think is most accurate and why? A challenge like facing terminal cancer will...

a. make you grow.

b. make you regress.

c. reveal who you are.

9. Too Hard to Pray

Some things are just harder to pray than others. In the third petition of what is commonly called the Lord's Prayer, Jesus taught us to pray the words, "Your will be done on earth as it is in heaven" (Matthew 6:10). For me, that became almost too hard to pray during the cancer journey.

Right at the beginning of our cancer journey I asked people to pray for God's will to be done, whether that meant healing or heaven. I remember sitting at my computer wrestling with that. When I first wrote those words to e-mail them to our praying friends, it took me quite some time to write them down. I knew I ought to pray God's will be done, and that other people should pray that for us. Yet it was hard to be honest and still ask then to pray that. I was praying the prayer more out of duty than desire. Why? Because I wanted God's will to be done, yes, but only "if" his will being done was actually the same or very close to the same as my will being done. And my will was very clear at this point. It was for Mary to find healing and stay with me, my partner in life for a long, long time.

More than halfway through the cancer journey, I wrestled with that prayer again. The question of Mary's future was becoming less clear to me. I still knew God could heal her, and was usually certain he would heal her, and we were thankful for how well she was still doing. But it was clear he had not healed her yet. It was clear that cancer was still advancing.

The Balcony and the Road

In his excellent little book, *Suffering and God*, Alister McGrath entitles the first chapter, "The Balcony and the Road." He borrows the imagery from a theologian, John Mackey, who spent many years in Spain in the 1920s. The imagery of the balcony and the road are used to illustrate the fact that there are two very different ways of looking at the things that happen in life. McGrath writes, "By the Balcony...I mean that little platform in wood or stone that protrudes from the upper window of a Spanish home. There the family may gather...to gaze spectator-wise upon the street beneath, or at the sunset or the stars beyond.... By the Road, I mean the place where life is tensely lived, where thought has its birth in conflict and concern, where choices are made and decisions are carried out. It is the place of action, of pilgrimage, of crusade, where concern is never absent from the wayfarer's heart. On the Road a goal is sought, dangers are faced, life is poured out. The two different perspectives are those of the spectator and the participant."[17]

---

[17] Alister McGrath, *Suffering and God*, Grand Rapids, Michigan, Zondervan, 1992, p.11.

Do you see where I am going with this? I think I was moving a little further from the balcony and toward the road by the time I went through a second season of wrestling with that prayer. I began to know a reality in that prayer I had not known before. I was praying it at a different level.

Let me hasten to add, I'm not talking about having arrived in my experience of that prayer. I'm just talking about sensing a movement, and I think God is okay with us noticing when there is movement. It is movement He notices keenly.

So I resumed praying "Your will be done," and it was prayed in a deeper way than before. I still felt free to ask God for what I really wanted, for Mary to be healed of cancer. But now I was just sharing with my "Abba" (Aramaic for "beloved dad") the desire of my heart. And now, I was again praying "Your will be done," but with less of a feeling that His will just had to be similar to mine. On the long and difficult road, I was becoming okay with His will being His.

In God's School of Prayer

God "took me to school" in regards to that kind of praying about two years earlier. I believe he was preparing me for what lay ahead. The lesson was about wanting something badly, beginning to seriously doubt God is going to give it to you, and ending up being okay with it either way.

For our 35th Anniversary, we decided to go on an Alaskan cruise. So we made arrangements, prepaid, booked our flights to Vancouver and anticipated the trip. We arrived at the airport a full two hours before flight time. Big mistake. The line-up at baggage check was the longest I had ever seen it. It was moving very slowly. By the time we reached the check in, I figured we had about fifteen minutes to spare. We gave the lady our information and she shocked us with, "Didn't anyone talk to you in the line-up? Your flight has been cancelled." I explained about the cruise which we had prepaid. She said the best she could do was get us on the next flight. We took a quick glance at the flight information, nervously booked it, and watched our luggage go out of sight.

We got through security, sat down, and began to think about how we'd get from Vancouver Airport to the docks. It suddenly became clear to me that the flight we had just booked was going to get us there about half of an hour too late.

But on the overhead screens I could see there was an earlier flight, leaving in less than an hour. So I spent the next three quarters of an hour in line ups, trying to get ticket agents to switch our flight. It was disconcerting to see "walk-ons" getting on the flight we wanted, while we were shuffled aside because no one wanted to do the leg-work of getting our luggage re-routed. I got the distinct impression they just didn't want to bother. I kept pushing at that flight until the doors closed, and it was gone.

Now what? I was on the phone with my travel agent and she noticed another flight that was leaving in about an hour, but would actually arrive in Vancouver a bit earlier than the one we had just missed. It was a direct flight, and would get us there just in time to maybe catch a taxi to the docks. I should try to switch to that flight.

So, back to line ups. I explain my situation to another agent, and I am surprised to find a most helpful ticket agent. Darryl started to work on it on two levels, baggage and tickets. He was immediate and he was insistent. He was on the phone non-stop. He kept calling, first one person then another. He phoned about ten people, while I stood there, glued to every word.

He finally said to me, "Look, Bert, I'm going to keep working on this until I get somewhere. Why don't you just sit over there where I can see you, and I'll give you the nod when I make some progress." So I sat next to Mary and explained what was happening. I'd been chasing flights for about two hours now. She asked me if I was okay. No doubt she'd been praying for me. My fuse wasn't as short as it used to be, but it could still be short. I told her that I was doing all right, but I wanted those tickets so badly it hurt.

"I've got TWO!"

We were waiting for a nod from Darryl, and for the first time, I thought to pray about it. I told God exactly what was happening, and how special Mary was to me, and how I really wanted us to make that boat. And then I crossed a bit of a milestone in my brief conversation with God. I also told him that I was okay with not making it if for some reason He didn't want us to sail. I actually told Him that. Then I said I believed He could still open a way for us if He wanted us to be on that ship. It wasn't a long prayer. It was short and it was sincere. I remember exactly how I ended the prayer. It was one of those prayer-moments I will never forget. "Lord," I said, "I know You can still open a way for us, but if You are going to do it, You'll have to do it right about now."

I opened my eyes, looked toward the ticket counter, and Darryl was just turning to look at me. He had the biggest grin on his face as he mouthed the words, "I've got you TWO!" "Thank You, Lord," I whispered.

The way it all went down, even though we paid for it, we always looked at that cruise as a gift. And I often thought about that brief prayer time. It was a powerful lesson on wanting something very badly, yet being okay with things if it was not God's will. I think it was instrumental in my being able to honestly pray for God's will during the cancer journey. Only now the stakes were much higher. I was praying about something I wanted much more than a plane ticket.

Deeper on the Road

About a month before Mary died, I began wrestling with that prayer at a deeper level still. It was only now becoming clear to me that unless God miraculously intervened, Mary was going to die. No one had said that to us, but we could read the pity in the eyes of some of the doctors and nurses. It was happening more and more. I know I began to have a real sense of being at a fork-in-the-road time in our lives. It was now or never.

When it becomes now or never, you are forced to think about the never in clearer terms. I know I did. What if God did not heal her? What if that was not his will? It's one thing to pray, "Your will be done" as a spectator, quite another to pray as a participant "on the road." But it is deeper again to pray those words when it becomes clearer that He actually might not give you what you most want. It's not a quick thing; at least it wasn't for me. It was more like a season of prayer, and a growing awareness.

Help from the Example of Jesus

In the middle of that season, Easter Sunday of 2012, I was particularly blessed by a thought Pastor Baker shared in a sermon at Calvary Baptist Church in Oshawa, our home church. Pastor Rick was talking to us about the experience of Jesus in the Garden of Gethsemane, when Jesus was the one praying that exact prayer, "Your will be done." Remember how the story is told in the gospels? Jesus went to pray by himself three times, "Father, if it is possible, let this cup pass from me." But three times he also added, "Yet not as I will, but as You will."

Pastor Rick pointed out something significant in the wording of Matthew's account in 26:39-42. The first time Jesus prayed those words, he said, "If it is possible, may this cup be taken from me. Yet not as I will, but as you will." The words change however, in verse 42, and to Pastor Rick the change is significant. "He went away a second time and prayed, 'My Father, if it is *"not"* possible for this cup to be taken away unless I drink it, may your will be done." (Emphasis, mine).

Rick pointed out that there was a deepening awareness revealed by the words of Jesus. By the second time he prayed, he was becoming more aware that God *was not* going to provide another way. He was becoming fully aware that he would indeed drink the cup of suffering. Yet knowing full well what that would mean for Him, he still prayed "Your will be done."

I left that worship service comforted by the fact that Jesus was my Pioneer on exactly this difficult road of prayer. And so I prayed that prayer on a deeper level once again. Remember, I'm not talking in terms of having "arrived" but in terms of "movement". I did pray it again, and I know that this time it was much harder to pray.

It was hard for Jesus too. When Jesus prayed it knowing full well what was to come, he exhibited severe stress for perhaps the first time in his life. The Bible tells us the stress was so severe that he was sweating as it were drops of blood. That strongly impresses upon me that praying "Your will be done," is never meant to be shallow or easy. A deep prayer is almost never an easy prayer, is it?

Until I was Okay with It

By the time Mary died, I was okay with it. Don't get me wrong, it's not what I wanted. Never in a thousand lifetimes! With all my heart it's not what I wanted. I loved her more than ever before. My whole being wanted her to live.

But at the same time, I was okay with her dying. I was at peace with it. I wasn't fighting God at all on it anymore. I was partly just too exhausted to fight but mostly had grown to accept God's will in the matter. So in that sense, I was okay with it.

It was only on the last day of Mary's life that I stopped even "asking" God to heal her. She was in a semi-coma. Now I was praying about home-going instead of healing. I knew God still could heal her, but for the first time, I was quite sure He was not going to. So I began to pray that if He was going to take her home, He would do it peacefully and gently, and that she would be spared much pain. Now I was no longer asking God to be her Healer. Now I was asking Him to be her Shepherd on these last few steps of the walk that led her truly home.

REFLECTION

1. Think carefully and prayerfully before you answer this question. Are you more on the "balcony" or more on "the road" when it comes to this prayer (Your Will Be Done)?

2. How could staying on the "balcony" be something that robs you of blessing?

3. Do you think we should ask for the "road", or do you think it's something that's bound to come? If so, what should we be asking God for?

4. Do you agree with my assertion that it is okay to notice positive movement in our own

spiritual status?   How can we keep this from becoming a pride thing?

5. Should, "Your will be done," as a deep, on-the-road prayer be an easy prayer to pray? If it is not easy, am I somehow displaying a lack of faith? Why or why not?

6. Some theologians have concluded that praying about God's "will" is more about changing us than Him? Do you know of any Scriptures that would support such a conclusion?

10. Walking Mary Home

It took me a long, long time to write about Mary's home-going -- about six months before I could even begin and well over a year before I finished. The memories are so close to my heart, I can hardly think back to those days without tears. They are not all tears of sadness.

Let me start by talking to you about some difficult decisions. They came about because of a very unexpected turn of events. Mary had been doing so well up until the end of April, 2012. Then she started to cough a lot. She just couldn't seem to stop, and it began to hurt her so much. Cancer was creeping into her diaphragm. We took her for some tests, including a lung scan, to rule out a suspected blood clot.

What doctors found instead was pneumonia in her right lung. She was given a fairly high-powered antibiotic. It was good for the pneumonia, but unfortunately very bad for her stomach. She suddenly couldn't eat much of anything anymore, and began to lose weight dramatically. Her skin and eyes began to significantly yellow--signs that her liver was failing. The last scan was so painful for her that we asked our doctor to do no more tests. It was a difficult decision. It felt like the end of the line as far as modern medicine goes.

The doctor began to make house calls, helping us to prepare for looking after Mary at home. She was gracious, going far beyond the expected in caring for Mary. She gave us her pager number and didn't just ask us, but insisted we call any time, day or night, if there was a change or we had a question. We were grateful for her care. More and more equipment began to arrive. It seemed like every day brought something new.

That brings up one of the more difficult decisions we had to make. We were suddenly faced with the fact that Mary might be dying. I didn't actually think so, and I wouldn't have believed it was possible a week before, but things had suddenly turned serious. We talked about the issue of dying at home, and whether or not that was what she wanted. My main concern was that we'd be able to keep her comfortable enough. But I was committed to keeping her at home as long as that is where she wanted to be.

Mary's concern was especially for her grandchildren. Our home was their home too. And Mary didn't want our grandsons, Noah and Joel to remember our home as the place where she died. So she wanted to stay at home as long as possible, but she did not want to die there. It was just one more sacrifice she was glad to make for her beloved grandsons. They were that kind of special to her.

We did everything we could to keep her comfortable. The day shift was looked after by our daughters and Mary's sisters. I did the night shifts. We filled the house with conversation and love. Tons of good food was brought to us. People came to visit and pray with us. Lots of good music and words filled our home.

I was gone during the days, but in the evening, when it was just the two of us again, I'd get her all relaxed. I'd often pull out the guitar and play and sing with Mary. She sometimes couldn't sing out loud, because it made her cough again. But even then she was softly humming or least singing with her eyes. We'd do the whole bath and massage routine. And through it all, we still managed to sleep very peacefully, except when she began to cough.

Spring was in the air so we still tried to walk. She couldn't do our driveway anymore or any hill. So I'd get her into the Ford Escape, and we'd drive up to the Crown Land and walk level bits of the trails she loved so much. Our love-walk had come full circle. We had started slow. We had picked up speed for most of our years together, but now we were ambling again, still firmly hand in hand.

The Night Shift Gets Harder

Sunday, May 27, 2012 was the first very difficult night shift. There had been some challenges in the nights before, but this one was in another league. We started off in our own bed for a few hours. When that got too uncomfortable for Mary, we shifted her to the hospital bed downstairs while I dozed on the couch.

The next night was even worse. Between her coughing and discomfort, neither of us really got any sleep at all. Neither our bed nor the hospital bed remained comfortable for more than a few moments. Pillows and back-rubs and pain killers were little help. We went back and forth between the two beds all night long. I could hardly get her up and down the stairs anymore. She was losing all her strength. I almost had to carry her.

She wasn't in acute pain. It was just a complete lack of comfort. We were not sure if it was the pneumonia or if it was her liver failing. It was the roughest night yet. And it proved to be our last night alone together.

In the morning, I managed to get her up and showered and dressed. I was barely able to get it done. She was too weak and nauseous to eat anything that morning.

By then, Mary had become too weak to read. Jenn had given her Sarah Young's devotional, *Jesus Calling*. It was one of the devotional books Mary had been reading since the New Year. On sick days like these, the girls were reading from it to Mary.

That morning, Sara read to her, "I AM WITH YOU, watching over you constantly. I am Emmanuel *(God with you)*; My presence enfolds you in radiant love. Nothing, including the brightest blessings and the darkest trials, can separate you from Me. Some of My children find me more readily during dark times, when difficulties force them to depend on Me.... I know precisely what you need to draw nearer to Me. Go through each day looking for what I have prepared for you. Accept every event as My hand-tailored provision for your needs. When you view your life this way, the most reasonable response is to be thankful. Do not reject any of My gifts; find Me in every situation."[18]   Mary accepted those words as a personal message from God. It was how she went into the day.

We called a family conference first thing that morning. With our full agreement, Mary decided she should go to the hospital for a few days and hopefully get her strength pumped back up a bit. We were not really thinking about death, at least I wasn't. I'm quite sure Mary actually knew. She had said as much to the girls in the last day or two. I was hoping a few days of intravenous treatments would let her stomach settle down so she could take some nourishment again, and that her coughing would be able to be controlled for a period. I was hoping she'd be home again in less than a week.

A Tough Ride

The ride to the hospital was absolutely horrible. It's the only way I can describe it. Why all ambulances don't have air-ride suspensions is hard for me to understand. Something so simple and

---

[18] Sarah Young, Jesus Calling, Nashville, Tennessee, Thomas Nelson, 2004, page 156.

inexpensive would have made such a difference for Mary. In looking back I wish we had just taken one of our own cars. It would have been much more comfortable for Mary, even though getting her in and out would have been a major challenge.

I didn't know an ambulance could be so rough. The stretcher was hard as a rock. Every bump on the road jarred Mary's body. I was riding in the back with her, stuffing pillows around her and trying to keep her body from rocking too hard against the rails of the stretcher. She was seat-belted in place fairly tightly. I threw off my seatbelt so I could reach her to try to keep her more comfortable. I kept asking for more pillows until I had them all in play. It seemed impossible, however, to ease her ride. By the time we got to the hospital, she was pale and exhausted, fighting back tears.

I remember watching the road fade away from us through the back window and wondering if this might be our last ride together. We held hands, and often locked eyes and whispered "I love you" to one another. She was still able to bravely smile at me, but it felt like the longest fifteen minutes of our life. The doctor had arranged for Mary to be admitted into room 105 at the Mooseport hospital. She arrived just after two o'clock in the afternoon on May 29.

The nurses were great. They very quickly got her more comfortable than we could at home. Then it was just her and me for a few minutes before the rest of the family arrived. Throughout that afternoon, many people came and went, and were able to connect with Mary. She had just occasional discomfort.

The Spirit of Room 105

The room was usually fairly full, but it was never hectic or on edge. Maybe it was because God had graciously enabled both Mary and I to be relaxed with what was happening. Maybe it was because many people were praying for us. In spite of the fact that it was a hospital room, it was a good place to be. A spirit of love and gentleness took over there. That Presence we had been reading about earlier in the day was very much in-house. There was laughter and there was conversation. There was joy mingled with tears every time another person said, "I'll see you later."

Mary would occasionally doze off, but she was mostly awake and smiling and talking. Even though she knew she was face to face with the last enemy, death, she was facing it so well. There wasn't even a hint of fear in her. Instead there was peace. The room was permeated with peace. I don't think it was drug-induced either. I'm sure it was Spirit-given. As I re-live that day, I think I would even call Mary "noble." For the last year and a half, I had been her warrior. By now she had become my "warrior- princess."

Once visiting hours were over, it was just Mary and me and our children again. We decided that since we didn't know how things would go, we should never leave Mary alone. Two of us would always be there to help her if need be, and just to keep her company. We split up the week into shifts. It was Adam and his girlfriend, Lacey who would take the first shift. I was beyond tired. Around ten o'clock, I kissed Mary good-night and went home to sleep. She wanted me to go. I didn't know then that it would be our last mutual kiss. From now on, I would be doing the kissing. She could no longer reciprocate.

I found out the next day that in the middle of the night, Sara and Jenn both woke up thinking about their Mom, and unable to fall back asleep, they went back to the hospital. For much of that night, four of her children were with Mary. Back at home, after a shower and a very brief time of prayer, I fell into a much needed and peaceful, but brief sleep.

May 30, 2012

I returned to the hospital early the next morning, relieved to learn that Mary had slept very peacefully too. However, sometime during that night, her sleep turned into a semi-coma. She couldn't open her eyes in the morning. We could see her responding to us when we talked to her. Her eyelids would flutter a bit, like she was trying to open them. But she just didn't have the strength. And her mouth would form the tiniest bit of a smile when we talked to her as well. So we knew she could hear us, and we always assumed that day that she was listening. We didn't talk "about" her, but "to" her.

Our doctor came frequently to check on us. As head of the palliative care team at the hospital, she talked to us privately about the process of death once a person falls into a coma. She told us that people are all very different in how they want to die. She said that even though they might say they don't, when it comes right down to it, many people actually want to die alone. They hang on to life as long as they sense someone they love is there, but choose to let life go when they feel they are alone. So she advised us, for as long as Mary was unable to wake up, to give her some time alone every hour.

Therefore all that day, we would leave her by herself for ten minutes of every hour. I told the kids that I didn't actually think Mary wanted to die alone, but that we should do what the doctor suggested, provided we made it very clear to Mary that we were never abandoning her. So we never just left her without telling her. We would talk right into her ear, telling her that we loved her, and that the doctor had advised us to give her a little time alone every hour. We were giving her a rest for a few minutes, and we would soon be back. We would always give her our "permission" to die, telling her we didn't *want* her to go, but if she sensed this was her time to go home, she should go with our blessing and love. We would see her later.

That day was almost the same as the day before with many people coming and going. The big difference is that Mary was slowly drifting deeper into coma. Most of Mary's siblings were able to connect with her one more time. Many who loved her came and spent a little time with us. Through it all, I'm sure Mary was conscious of us, although she continued to appear to be asleep.

The only thing that seemed to disturb her was that she would have a short time of the hiccups every hour or so. They made her groan a little every time it happened. The hiccups had started the day before, but were getting more pronounced. It seemed to bother her more. They gave her some medication to try to relax her diaphragm and that seemed to help.

My sister Judy and her husband Andy had come by in the middle of the afternoon, and then returned home. Around supper time, we felt we wanted to sing for Mary. We phoned Judy and asked her to come back with her guitar. She and Andy left their supper sitting on the table, brought the guitar, and we closed the door so as not to disturb others, and quietly sang for Mary. We sang for about half an hour, and we could tell she loved the music. Her mouth and body would move a bit to the songs. She was responding, but it seemed to be through a barrier, a veil of some kind. It felt like she wanted to wake up fully and be with us, but she couldn't. Love, prayers, hugs and a feeling of peace continued to fill the atmosphere in room 105, tinged with a very real cloud of sadness.

Throughout the day Mary was usually comfortable. She would occasionally get restless, but then I would lean in close to her and talk into her ear for a while and stroke her hair and face. She would almost immediately calm down and be restful again.

There was a lot of déjà vu to that scene for me and for others on her side of the family. A few years before, Mary's dad had suffered a stroke. He was hospitalized and at first it had seemed like it was a minor thing. But the bleeding in his brain never stopped, and he got worse as the day wore on. A large number of his family gathered around that hospital room. As he slipped from consciousness Mary's mom rarely left his side. In the hours before he died, Dad would frequently get very restless, and no one could calm him like Mom. Mom would lean in and stroke his face and talk to him and almost immediately he would be calm and at peace again. It was a beautiful testament of love to us their children and grandchildren. Mary and I later would thank Mom for leaving us such a legacy. She knew how to love her spouse to the end. Now it felt like that torch had been passed.

As evening drew near there were fewer and fewer loved ones, until it was just Sara and Jenn and me with Mary. They were on for the night shift; I was just staying as long as I could. I was getting utterly exhausted, knowing I needed to sleep, but feeling like I was abandoning Mary to do so. What if this was her time to go?   I was so torn between wanting to be there for her, yet knowing I was getting more useless to her by the moment.

We tried to get a sense from the nurses as to how Mary was doing. They seemed sure Mary was indeed dying. Her feet were beginning to swell even more than they had been for the last weeks. But the nurses were also quite sure that it would not happen for a while, probably not for days. Her pulse and breathing were both quite steady and strong. I decided to go home, have a quick rest, and be back early in the morning in better shape to be by her side again.

I kissed Mary and spoke into her ear for a while. I told her I was going home to try to get some rest. I told her again that I loved her and how glad I was to be her husband. I gave her my blessing to go and be with her Lord if He was calling her home. I told her that Sara and Jenn would be here through the night and I would be back in a few hours. Then I said, "I'll see you later," and "I love you very much." A final kiss, and a group hug with Jenn and Sara, and I left the room.

In fifteen minutes, I was home and after a brief prayer for Mary and all our children, I immediately fell asleep. It was just after ten o'clock. Within twenty minutes, the phone rang. It was Sara. She and Jenn had just come back from a walk around the block, leaving Mary alone for those minutes as we had been doing. She phoned because there seemed to be something different in the way Mary was breathing. It was more ragged, and she was suddenly more restless than she had been before. Her legs and arms had been mostly quiet all day, but now they were moving, like she was trying to walk, or grab something in a dream. She and Jenn had tried to calm Mary down, but it didn't seem to have any effect.

I was in a fog. So tired. I asked what the nurses thought was happening? They hadn't talked to the nurses yet. So I suggested they talk to them, get their opinion, see if Mary calmed down in five minutes, and then call me back. I told Sara I would pray about whether I should come in right now.

I found out later she was rather annoyed with me, not wanting me to pray but to come. I lay there for a few minutes, praying. Sara called back. She told me the nurses thought it was nothing significant, that Mary's pulse and breathing were still strong, and that I should not come in, but just get some needed rest.

Nevertheless, while Jenn wasn't sure, Sara was quite adamant. She told me she thought the nurses were wrong, and that something was happening. Sara had checked Mary's feet and noticed they were even more swollen, and their color had gone blotchy. Mary's sister Nancy, a nurse, had told Sara that was one of the signs of impending death. So to convince me, Sara held the phone near Mary and I could hear the difference in her breathing.

The main thing bothering Sara is that her Mom wasn't calming down, the restlessness was getting worse even though they had increased her morphine drip to "2" and given her some Ativan.

I knew if anyone could calm her, it was me. So I told the girls I'd be there in fifteen minutes.

I was wearing my running shoes when I entered the hospital. I had been wearing those shoes all along during Mary's time there. You know how some shoes seem to walk noisily on certain floors? Mine did, on the floors of Mooseport hospital. They squeaked so loudly it was almost embarrassing. I actually tried to modify my gait so they would tone down a bit.

So there I was, squeaking my way down the hallway toward room 105 in the middle of the night. The door was ajar, and upon entering, I found to my surprise that Mary wasn't restless at all. Her breathing, arms and legs were all completely calm. And the girls had a stunned look on their faces because Mary had been more restless than ever until the exact moment my feet crossed the threshold of the door. It was like my first squeaky footstep into the room had activated a calming switch in Mary.

I believe Mary had been waiting for me. Mary just wanted me to be there. Finding a way to get me there was her love-gift to me. She knew how much I needed to be there. It was her beloved intuition at work once again. Her restlessness was the only way she had to communicate a message to the girls that said, "Get Bert!" As soon as she heard my footstep she knew I was there and no longer needed to send that message. Mature love is like that. It finds a way to communicate something even when it is impossible to speak.

I also believe it was a God-thing. It was God who orchestrated a way to make sure I was there, because He knew I needed to be there. Someone wanted me there. I'm glad I arrived exactly when I did. I think both possibilities were probably at work.

I went to Mary's side, kissed her, and talked into her ear for a while.

I wasn't tired anymore. I was completely alert, alive to the moment. The girls were a little bit giddy. The furniture was fairly sparse in the room. There was a chair and a cot. They knew I was coming so they wanted another chair. They had gone into the hall and found this odd chair on wheels that looked like it was made to be able to move a very large person around. I mean big-Bertha-large! They had looked both ways, borrowed it, squeezed it through the door, and found it was large enough for both of them to sit side by side. So they were on one side of Mary in their giddy chair, and I was on the other, as we talked to her.

We talked for a while, and then in a moment of silence, the words of an old hymn suddenly came to my mind. So I thought, "She loves worship so much. Why not sing to her?" It was an older hymn, written in the late 1800's, and I didn't think the girls would know it, so I just started to sing to Mary,

"Softly and tenderly Jesus is calling, calling for you and for me;

See, on the portals, He's waiting and watching, watching for you and for me.

Come home, come home, ye who are weary come home.

Earnestly, tenderly, Jesus is calling, calling oh, (Mary), come home."

(Will L. Thompson, 1847-1909)

The girls only half knew the song. They were trying to sing along, but it reminded me of the Mr. Bean episode where he is trying to sing along in church, when he doesn't know the words or the tune. They were always about half a word and half a note behind me. It was actually a bit humorous.

After the song it was quiet for a while. The girls were on one side, holding her hand. I was on the other.

We sat and held her hands for a few moments. She was completely peaceful, no longer ragged in her breathing, but shallow, consistent and quiet. I could feel her gentle, steady pulse in my hand.

I suddenly knew I needed to pray. That knowledge just welled up in me. If you've spent much time praying, you probably know what I'm talking about. Sometimes the Spirit calls you to pray, and He usually does it by making you "just know" you have to pray.

So I said to the girls, "Let's pray together." I stood at Mary's side, leaning over her, holding her right hand in mine. I don't normally do this, but I felt I should place my other hand on her forehead. So I put my left hand gently on her brow, almost like a priestly blessing was being bestowed on her. I began to quietly pray over her, first of all, a prayer of gratitude.

"Lord, I thank you so much for Mary. I thank you for her life and for her love. Thank you so much for the gift of love you have placed between us. Thank you God, for how she has enriched my life, and I have been able to enrich hers. Now, here we are, in this place and at this moment in our lives. We confess before you that we really don't know what is happening here right now. But we're thankful that you know. We rest in that. We don't know if this is Mary's time to go home to be with you or not. You know it's the last thing on earth we want. You know that with all our hearts we wish we could keep her here. But if this is her time to go, then we're okay with it, Lord. And we have just one request. Would you please just take her gently? Please, ease her there? Lord, we want to confess that we love you and trust you even now. Amen."

I suddenly realized that sometime in the middle of that brief prayer, I had stopped feeling a pulse. It was no longer there. It had happened so quietly I had not even noticed. I looked more closely and she wasn't breathing anymore. I knew she was gone. I had walked her home. By the grace of God's timing, my prayer had carried her the last few steps of her journey. There was peace.

Mary had come home.

REFLECTION

1. Before you reflect on any of these questions, take a few moments to pray. This chapter has invited you to share in a very sacred moment. I now ask you to take a little time to talk to God before moving on. Write down a few of your own prayer-thoughts.

2. If you had a terminal illness, would you want to die at home?   Why or why not?

3. Do you think a family "owes" it to a person to fulfill their requests in this area?

4. Do you think the whole restlessness/squeaky-shoe event was...

a. a Mary thing

b. a God thing

c. other

Why?

5. What aspects of Mary's home-going stand out to you as particular blessings?

6. How was it nevertheless a curse?

11. Celebrating Mary's Walk

Mary died just before midnight on Wednesday, May 30, 2012. I asked our doctor to phone the funeral home, and we went home and tried to get some sleep.

The next few days are a blur of activity. We met as a family on Thursday morning, and decided we wanted to try to have the funeral on Saturday. It was a bit of a rush, and the funeral director was worried we wouldn't be able to get the word out in time for a visitation and the service. I told him I didn't think that would be a problem. I was confident our e-mail prayer chain would get the word out, and it did. There were about five hundred people who came to pay their respects to the family, and over five hundred the next day for her funeral. About a month after the funeral, I sent out a final e-mail to our prayer chain. It was a transcript of Mary's funeral. The e-mail (slightly abbreviated) which I sent out follows.

July 2, 2012.

It is already a month since Mary graduated to God's presence. I had intended to send this update a lot sooner, but have been struggling with it, procrastinating because I think I unconsciously knew it would not be easy. Writing this update feels so final, like it really is the last goodbye or something. So this has been written through many tears. But tears or not, I wanted to write this to you all for three reasons. First, a number of people told me they were deeply touched by the Service of Remembrance and Celebration for Mary. They wished they could have the text so they could read and think again about the things that were said.

Second, I know also a number of people very much wanted to be there but couldn't. So for them, I write.

And finally, I write for myself. It makes Mary's absence more bearable to think that the cancer journey and her passing can actually be an ongoing influence for good in our lives. She lived well, she loved well, and she died well. Her life is an encouragement to all of us. So here is the text, sent out with the prayer that through it, Mary's life would continue to speak into ours.

The service began with prayer, and the reading of Scripture. We then sang together a song that had meant a lot to Mary, "He Knows My Name."

"I have a Maker, He formed my heart,

Before even time began, my life was in his hands.

Chorus: He knows my name, He knows my every thought

He sees each tear that falls, and hears me when I call.

I have a Father, He calls me His own.

He'll never leave me, No matter where I go."

That was followed by a slideshow, pictures of Mary and her family. (Many of the pictures were a wonderful gift. A few days after Mary's cancer surgery, a long-time friend of our son Nathan's, Jeff Marchant phoned. He had lost his mom a few years earlier to bowel cancer, and always regretted they did not have more good pictures of her. Since that time he has become a professional photographer [a good one too]. He didn't want us to be left with that same regret so he told us he was coming over to do a family shoot. We went to the lakefront and into the woods behind our house, and he took some of the most amazing photos. They are a family treasure. Many of the slides were from that photo shoot.) The slideshow was set to some of Mary's favorite songs, and was a beautiful walk through her life and our memories of her.

Two of Mary's sisters then shared some remembrances on behalf of all her siblings.

Joanne: "I am Joanne and this is Nancy. We have the privilege of representing our siblings to tell you about our beautiful sister, Mary. Mary was the second of eight children born to Joe and Kathleen. She was a tiny little girl who was the apple of her dad's eye. As the oldest sister Mary always had a motherly way about her. She was always loving, and always concerned about her siblings. Mary loved order and cleanliness. She could often be found in the kitchen cleaning messes left by her sisters and brother.

"I was blessed to have a special relationship with Mary from an early age. Our oldest brother, Richard, died when I was just six months old. Mary stepped in to care for me when grief was just too much for our parents. She became more than a sister to me; she was like my second mom.

"As the little girls of the family, we have no real recollection of when Bert entered our family because we were too young. We just heard you made quite an impact! But seriously, that impact was a wonderful thing for our whole family. Bert, you could always bring a twinkle to Mary's eye and a smile to her face. After they married, Bert and Mary would always welcome you into their home. They would take time to visit with you and more often than not, feed you.

"As our family grew up and were married off, Mary was a wonderful example for us to follow. She was always there to give advice, to tell you 'This too shall pass,' when parenting frustrations set in. Mary would step in and take your children so you could rest, come to clean when you couldn't, or pray for whatever need your family had.

"She was the first to welcome new members to our family with a great big hug and kiss... whether they were ready or not! Mary was a 'less talk, more action' kind of person. She could often be heard at our family get-togethers saying, 'OK, people! Let's make a decision and just do it!'

"Her kids were the joy of her life. And her grandchildren... well, let's just say we did not have a conversation without her mentioning something Noah or Joel said or did."

Nancy: "In the last year of her life Mary often surprised us. She didn't complain, or say, 'Why me?' and her strong faith was so evident. No matter what was happening, she still had such joy when you talked to her.

"Cancer takes a lot of things from us, but one thing it does give... time to say the things you always wanted to say to your loved ones. As a family I think we all had the privilege of being able to tell Mary how we felt about her and what she meant to us. When we asked Mary how she felt about this journey, she made it very clear that she was at peace and knew that one day she would be in heaven with our Lord. Mary spoke very openly about our loved ones who have gone to see the Lord before her. She joked in her sibling humor of the fact that there is a benefit to being the oldest, and being the first to go so she gets to see Dad first. Mary loved children, and we can't help but think that there is no better person to be with our children in heaven than Mary. She shared one day with us that she had a vision of hugging Richard, Mark,

Megan, Rebecca and Chloe[19] at heaven's gate. Thank you for that gift, Mary, a gift we will always carry with us.

"From the moment Mary was diagnosed with cancer, Bert and Mary's home became a place everyone was welcome to visit, at any time. Never once did you feel like you were intruding into their lives. We as siblings took turns travelling to Mary's house, sometimes with very heavy hearts. But by the time we left, Mary and Bert and their children had lifted our spirits in their own special way. That was such a blessing to all of us. Mary taught us how important family is, and how to live our lives with no regrets, and to be intentional in how we showed love. This intentional love is very apparent in her own family."

Nancy then turned to address Mary's children and grandchildren. "Nathan, Jenn, Noah, Joel, Sara, Adam, Aimee and Chris, you are an amazing family. Mary was so proud of you. You all honored her on a daily basis. You all took such good care of her. Bert, we want to say a special thank you for everything you have done. Your relationship with Mary was a beautiful example of what a marriage should be. In this last year we were able to witness how you expressed your love, from the hours of research to improve her daily quality of life, to the songs you sang to her, and how you cared for her

---

[19] Richard, Mary's older brother, died when he was fourteen. Mark, Megan, Rebecca and Chloe are young children our extended family has tragically lost.

basic needs. You tenderly cared for her. Thank you so much for loving our sister in so many ways."

Nancy and Joanne then left the stage, and our children, Nathan and Jenn, Adam, Sara, Aimee and Christopher stepped up to the platform. Nathan took the microphone and spoke on behalf of all of them. They had written this together the night before.

"It has been an honor and a blessing having our Mom for a Mom. We have been blessed each one of us to have such a special and close relationship with her. We would like to start by saying a huge thank you from us to our friends and family who have walked with us during this season of life...there are no words to say how much it means to us. Thanks for all the heartfelt prayers, food drop offs and special care for Noah and Joel. We couldn't have walked this journey without you...so please accept our sincere gratitude.

"From the beginning our mom knew how to love us unconditionally. If there was one thing we could count on when feeling down it was a hug and kiss or a comforting word to bring us back to reality. Our reality is that we have been utterly blessed to be surrounded by and loved by Mom. Mom was a love foundation that was unwavering. She loved us with every touch, every word and every prayer she said. Our mom was a great role model. She led by example with care and compassion, never complaining or asking for anything in return. Thank you Mom for your love; for all the wonderful times we could share, for all the dreams that came true and will come true because of your exceptional guidance and nurturing hand.

"We have so many memories of Mom loving Noah and Joel. She was a phenomenal Grandma. She was always so gentle with them; she always took such great care of them. She taught them all sorts of things that we would have never thought of, and she fed them. We can't count the times we would sit down to eat dinner and the boys wouldn't touch their dinner. When we would ask them what Grandma gave them for a snack a common response would be: a roll up, a cookie and then a bowl of ice-cream. It makes us think, 'Sure Mom fed them when they were little and didn't eat much, but what about in three years?' Dad, you better stock up!

"Mom left a legacy of love. She loved us when we weren't really lovable; she was the first to give us a hug. Even when she was initially diagnosed she was comforting us. Her prayers for us and our family have shaped who we are today and they will forever change us.

"You may not know this, but if you ever wanted to make Mom's face light up, just bring over a basket of laundry. Mom loved to do it. It didn't matter if it was your undies and bras or your favorite blanket, she wanted to wash it. We always wondered why she loved this so much. A few years ago one of us asked her why did she always want to do our laundry? She said it was her way of serving others. She would be thinking about the person who owned the clothing as she handled it. So it may sound crazy at first, but it isn't. Mom really did love doing it. Each shirt she folded (even if it was a little smaller than before the wash) was folded with love. For us, it was like wearing a big hug every day.

"Mom was, and still is, our source of strength. Her daily prayers for us uphold us even now. She was not only mentally strong; she was physically intimidating, just try to get away from her when you're in big trouble! Once the grip was locked, you weren't going anywhere—we learned pretty quickly to always listen to our momma! The emotional and physical strength she showed during her season of cancer was unbelievable; never complaining, always comforting us and squeezing our hands when our tears were falling on her. Her strength came from the Lord and she has passed her legacy onto us.

"It has been a privilege for us to walk beside her during her final season of life. She has implanted so much in our hearts and she will forever be missed. We love you Mom and we hope we've loved you well. We find peace that you are no longer in pain, dancing and singing with Jesus....praise the Lord....we will see you in Heaven Mom."

After the kids, I came to the platform. There were so many things I wanted to say. I could have spoken for a long time, but condensed my thoughts to say the following.

"Exactly forty years ago this month, Mary and I began to date one another. We have grown together in love ever since that time. We grew in love because we did the things that build love. We worked together, laughed together, learned together, walked together (always holding hands), served together, worshipped together and prayed together. She was my marriage partner, my business partner, my ministry partner and my closest friend. We raised our family together, renovated houses together and tended gardens together. We were living proof that as love is nurtured it grows deeper with time. Our love was still growing when she was called to eternal life, and our last moment together was rich in love.

"So a day like today would be almost unbearable except for two things. The first is this: I believe in the Love of GOD. Mary believed in that too. We both believed that God loves us. By the way I think that was foundational to our married love, because it freed both of us to just enjoy each other and love each other, not to need each other or to cling to each other. I believe in the love of God, and that right now he loves me and he loves my children and grandchildren, and that he loves our extended family. It doesn't mean we don't have grief and that we don't miss Mary. We do miss her and will always miss her. Our grief is real and very deep.

"And when you are faced with that it's one thing to say something; it's another to believe it. I believe in the love of God. I've believed in that for a long time. Mary and I both believed it. When her cancer was diagnosed, she didn't fall apart and she didn't retreat from life. Way back then we talked about some of those hard questions. Like, 'Why me?' It crossed my mind, and I immediately thought to myself, 'We live in a fallen world where sicknesses and diseases happen every day to people, whether they deserve them or not. So 'Why me?' is really the wrong question. The right question is, 'Why not me?' Why should I be excluded from the pain that comes from living in a world where not everything is right?'

"We were driving home from the hospital the very first day we found out about the cancer and I was thinking those things, so I turned to Mary, and asked her, "Mary, are you asking yourself, 'Why is this happening to us?' She didn't hesitate for a second. 'Why not to us, hon?' So we talked about it, and we decided that we'd never bother to ask that question again. Instead we'd just keep believing that God would love us through this circumstance. He loves her, he loves me, he loves us. And Mary is enjoying that love and living in that love right now. It's one thing to say something; it's another to believe it. I believe in the love of God.

"A second thing makes it bearable for me too. I believe in the *active* love of God. That is, I believe he's not just an aura of love around us, or an inner force within us, but an actual being, a person who is able to do things, and actually does things because of his love for us. He is able to do great things, even miracles. That is why right to the end; I was asking God for a miracle of renewed health in Mary. A lot of us believe that, and a lot of us were asking for that too.

"So believing that, shouldn't we be crushed that he didn't answer those prayers? Shouldn't we be kind of ticked at God right now? It wouldn't be the first time a person reacted like that from the disappointment of unanswered prayer.

"I choose not to react that way, because I know something else that's true about God's active love. The miracle of answered prayers is not the only sure sign of God's active love.

"Sometimes God's active love doesn't give you what you want the most. Sometimes, instead, he carries you through what you want the least." (I paused here and repeated that line.)

"He has carried Mary and me through the cancer journey. He doesn't need to carry Mary anymore. He is still carrying me today. That makes it bearable.

"So toward God, I am not angry but so very, very grateful. He gave us such a wonderful gift in Mary. She was the steady, honest, loyal and just downright likeable love center of our home.

"Proverbs 31:10 says, 'A wife of noble character, who can find? She is worth far more than rubies.' Mary was worth far more than that to us, so to God I speak a word of gratitude for her life and for allowing me to share so much of life with her. I celebrate that life." (I then looked to heaven as I said, "Thank you Lord!")

"I also want to say a word of gratitude to God's people. Your prayers and your care for us, especially during this cancer journey have been overwhelming. In fact, they have carried us far more than we may know. Very often you have been the hands and feet that God has used to do His carrying. So thank you from the bottom of our hearts for your prayers for Mary. Though many of them were not answered in exactly the way we longed for, they were answered in deeper ways, some of them known only to God. So thank you as well.

"Please stand with me if you are able, as I lead us in a prayer of gratitude to God, for the gift of Mary.

"Lord God, our Heavenly Father. You are the one who gave us Mary. You gave her to us as daughter, sister, wife, mother, grandmother and friend. It was such a good gift, for she lived well and she loved well. Through her, our lives were made rich in love. So to you, the giver, we express our deepest thanks. Thank you so much for the gift of Mary. Amen."

Soloist Annie Ronson then ministered to us with the song, "Blessings".

We had specifically asked for that song. The song had a special place in our hearts. Mary and I were sitting at home on a Sunday evening just a few weeks after we discovered her cancer. I wrote about it in our April 4, 2011 update.

> *Last night as our day was winding down we wanted to listen to some music. Usually we listen to Praise and Worship Sunday on Life 100.3 via the internet. But our high tech wasn't so high, so we turned on Galaxie, the Light instead. The very first song we heard was one that immediately gripped us. It is a new song by Laura Story, called "Blessings." (New Spring Publishing) In the last year it kind of became "our" song. Every time we heard it, we were reminded that God was accomplishing something in us and through us that was way bigger than Mary's cancer.*

The chorus in particular ministered to us so powerfully all through the cancer journey. It goes,

> *"'Cause what if Your blessings come through raindrops*
>
> *What if Your healing comes through tears?*
>
> *And what if a thousand sleepless nights*
>
> *Are what it takes to know You're near?*
>
> *What if my greatest disappointments*
>
> *Or the aching of this life*

Is the revealing of a greater thirst this world can't satisfy?

And what if the trials of this life

The rain, the storms, the hardest nights

Are Your mercies in disguise?"

Pastor Rick Baker then led us in a meditation on the love of God. He began by pointing out that the love between Mary and I was rooted in God's love, for God is love. "God most powerfully demonstrated that love by sending Jesus to this world to be our Savior. At a time like this funeral, that love of God is good news for the Michel family. A long time ago, Mary traded perishing for eternal life through God's love."

He reminded us that God's love is not a pampering love, but a perfecting love. And some, like Mary, get there sooner than others. We get to a place of God's complete make-over. We are his masterpiece, and when his workmanship is complete, we have finished the course.

All through the course, we can be assured that nothing can separate us from the love of God. Except one thing. We can refuse to accept his love. Rick then explained the simple truth of the gospel. Though we are born separated from God, by his death for us, as we place our faith in him, Jesus has purchased reunion with God, eternal life with Him. Eternal life means when we die, we don't just cease to exist. God couldn't love us if we didn't exist. But he says he loves us after we die. The life he gives us is eternal life.

Mary is fully realizing that total love of God right now! We asked for her healing. We wanted her body healed. God's love for her gave her much more than we asked for. What He gave her is eternal glory. Sickness and death were trying to separate Mary from the Lord, but He would have none of that!

Rick asked us to listen carefully then reminded us that we weren't made for healing, we were made for heaven. Our mortality (2 Corinthians 5:4-5) is to be swallowed up by life. God has made us for this very purpose.

He closed by affirming the ongoing message of Mary's life. To all of us, the people she loved, her message is this: "Choose life, by choosing God's love for us. Welcome Jesus to be our Savior."

I'm thankful for Rick's gentle but direct reminder. That is indeed the message Mary would have wanted us all to hear and rejoice in. We talked about her memorial service a week or so before she died. She wanted us to sing, and as she put it, "not to sing dirges". And she wanted us to talk about the love of Jesus, and how that love meant cancer never won! God did.

The congregation then sang an older hymn called, "The Solid Rock." The first verse goes:

"My hope is built on nothing less, than Jesus' blood and righteousness.

*I dare not trust the sweetest frame, but
wholly lean on Jesus' name.*

*On Christ the solid rock I stand, all
other ground is sinking sand.*

All other ground is sinking sand."

It was our request that the words of Romans
8:31-39 be read aloud as we walked in procession
from the auditorium. The kids and I had asked
Mary's sisters to be honorary pall-bearers during
this part of the service. It was so we could honor
the sisterhood which Mary had been such a
beautiful part of. So as the sisters escorted her up
the centre aisle, the following triumphant words
were read by Pastor Steve Cottrell.

> *"What then, shall we say in response to
> these things? If God is for us, who can be
> against us? He who did not spare his own
> Son, but gave him up for us all- how will he
> not also, along with him, graciously give us
> all things? Who will bring any charge
> against those whom God has chosen? It is
> God who justifies. Who then is the one who
> condemns? No one. Christ Jesus who
> died – more than that, who was raised to
> life – is at the right hand of God and is also
> interceding for us. Who shall separate us
> from the love of Christ? Shall trouble or
> hardship or persecution or famine or
> nakedness or danger or sword?... No, in all
> these things we are more than conquerors
> through him who loved us. For I am
> convinced that neither death nor life,*

neither angels nor demons, neither the
present nor the future, nor any powers,
neither height nor depth, nor anything else
in all creation, will be able to separate us
from the love of God that is in Christ Jesus
our Lord."

Following the service, the ladies of Calvary Baptist (along with help from some generous family members) served refreshments in the lower level of the church. The cemetery we would use was Pine Grove Cemetery in Prince Albert, just south of Port Perry. Since it was a thirty-minute drive, we felt it would be better to have refreshments first, then the interment service. There were so many people there from every part of life Mary and I had walked together. There were people there from our high-school days, from our Bible School days, neighbors, business friends, and people from every church we had been part of over the years.

There were so many people that our immediate family purposely scattered to different areas of the large room so people could talk to us without feeling like they were in a lineup. A great volume of words, good words, were spoken. I sometimes wish I had carried a hidden tape recorder so I could play them over again. We spent over an hour there with people before we had to go toward Port Perry. The time was rich in relationship.

The drive to the cemetery took about half an hour. The service there was brief. We prayed and read words of hope from the Bible. Then after a final prayer, I led off as we each took a flower from one of the beautiful arrangements that were there, and quietly placed it on her coffin. As I laid a single red rose at her feet, I was suddenly full of gratitude to God. I felt like I was the luckiest man on earth to have walked through life with Mary. I stood, and lifted a hand toward heaven, and softly whispered a prayer of gratitude, "Thank You, Lord, for giving me Mary."

REFLECTION

After Mary's funeral, one of our associate pastors, Kelvin, came to talk to me. He's a hugger, and gave me a big man-hug, the strong bear-hug kind. Then he took my hand, shook it firmly, and said, "Thank you Bert, for showing us what a *real* Christian funeral is like." We talked about a few other things. But what he said got me to thinking. I wondered what he meant by that. Please reflect on the following:

1. What do you think Kelvin meant? What is a "real" Christian funeral? How is it different from an "unreal" Christian funeral? How is it different from a non-Christian funeral?

2. Why are these fairly important questions to be able to answer clearly?

12. A Stone for Mary (and Me)

I wanted her stone to be special.

Not "showy" special. Not outstanding in how it appears. Not bigger than the stones around it. Not fancy pictures. It wasn't that kind of special I was looking for. No, I wanted her stone to "say" something. I wanted it to speak--first of all to me, as I would probably be the one person who sees the stone more than anyone else, and secondly to our children and grandchildren too, and to Mary's extended family.

I knew it was Mary's stone now, but it would one day be mine too. I wanted our stone to say something about love. If I had to boil down the most significant thing I remember about Mary, I'd have to use the word "love." The love she had for me was clean, simple, quiet, and steady. It was the single greatest treasure of my life. Because of her love, I consider myself rich. I wanted our stone to say something about that; to remind me of it every time I saw it.

I had been thinking about that for a while. And I remembered something about our love, and how central "walking" was to our love. We walked together a lot. We used to go for walks in the forest during our dating days. Those walks became much less frequent once the children were born. It just didn't work out very well with baby schedules and bedtimes. But we began to pick it up again after about ten years of marriage. It started when we lived in the semi in Port Perry. We would often walk the sidewalks after supper, and then come back to tuck the kids in for the night. Often talking, sharing our day, always hand in hand, sometimes not saying a thing, and just walking together.

When we moved to Trillium Valley, a whole new pattern of walking was established. The woods in the valley were full of cross-country skiing trails. They became our spot to walk. After lunch has always been my "slow" time of day. I'm not much good mentally for an hour or more. So we decided that would be good time to walk, and most days we walked the trails for an hour. We walked holding hands, often stopping for a quiet kiss. I can still picture those trails in my mind, and almost smell the Trilliums and ferns and moss.

In 1991 we moved north to Echo Bay. Mondays were my day off, and we'd get the kids off to school, go out for breakfast, and have an extended walk. We were five minutes from wilderness in almost any direction, so we'd pack a picnic lunch, hop in the car, park near some new spot to explore, and hike the trails around the many lakes. Most other days of the week we would walk the village around lunchtime.

Then from 1997 to 2003 there were the trails of Cambridge, Ontario. Old Hespeler, where we lived, has a unique grid of forest paths that wind their way behind houses and through hills and ravines. It was on the trails of Cambridge that I noticed a tree with a peculiar bend in its trunk. I pointed it out to Mary, and we stopped to look at it. The bark on the tree was very smooth. The way the trunk slanted made it a perfect tree to relax and "lean" on. I said to Mary, "Do you know what kind of tree this is?" She said no, and I told her it was a Kissing Tree. Then I gently leaned her against the trunk and showed her what that meant. After that, we almost always stopped for a while at that tree.

From Cambridge we moved back to the Port Perry area, to Scugog Island. There we lived right next to the Crown Land at the top of the Island. That became our new favorite walking spot. We walked those trails until the last weeks of Mary's life.

Walking together built up our love. So I wanted this statement along the top of the stone. "Walked together in love."

Truly we loved each other, but our love was not yet perfect. It was great, but it still had not achieved the Biblical vision for love between a man and wife – a love likened to the love of Christ for His bride, the Church (Ephesians 5:31). The Bible also tells us that love is one of the only things that endures, that is eternal. Other things disappear, but love remains (I Corinthians 13:8-13). It seems as if the earthly love we have is but the beginning, the seed of a higher love. So I added to the words along the top of our stone. It says, "Walked together in love, graduated to a higher love."

The very foundation of our love, and certainly the future of our love is bound up in what Jesus did for us on the cross. So on either side of those words, I had a symbol etched, the symbol of the cross. Those crosses are not meant as superstitious symbols; they are symbols of the real faith Mary and I shared. That's at the top of the stone.

Below those crosses and "walking" words I placed, in larger letters, our full names, the dates of our birth, and the date of Mary's death. Her name is on the left: "Maria Chrisstina (Molenaar)." Mine is on the right, "Bert Cornelius Michel." Centered between our names is a pair of wedding bands wrapped around another date, the year we were married, 1975. We were dating each other and married to each other for two-thirds of our lives. I wanted our stone to be a reminder that love can endure, that it really can be for a lifetime.

The Gift of a Bird

On the bottom, left-hand corner of the stone, I had a cardinal engraved.

Living at the top end of Scugog Island, our place was of course a great place to see and listen to many birds. There were many species that loved to visit the cedar hedge along our driveway, often blue jays, swallows, wrens, chickadees, robins, black birds and crows. Occasionally there would be hummingbirds and red cardinals.

It started either the first or second time Mary had chemotherapy. After an unsatisfactory sleep, she had been given a very pleasant wake-up call. She had been awoken by the most beautiful song of a cardinal. It was singing right outside our bedroom window. It felt to her like a gift, like the bird was singing encouragement to her. And it started a pattern. All through the summer of 2011, and into fall and winter, the same cardinal sang for Mary. We never fed it, or encouraged it. It just kept coming. It became her "get up" call. I would come in to our room to kiss her good-bye as I left for work, and she would snuggle in bed and wait for the song of the cardinal before she got up.

On weekends, she would point it out to me, and I'd be listening for the song as well. That bird was a most beautiful singer. As winter turned to spring, the cardinal was still outside our window almost every day. On her last day at home, it was her wake up call.

And then a strange thing happened. We would usually only get a visit from the cardinal in the morning. But on Tuesday, May 29th something out of the ordinary occurred. Together with Mary we had decided she should probably spend a few days in the hospital to get re-hydrated and over the pneumonia that had been bothering her.

Our doctor agreed and arranged for a transport ambulance to come and get her at two o'clock that afternoon. The attendants got Mary on board, and I climbed in the back with her for the ride to Mooseport.

Our kids would excitedly tell us later that as the ambulance made its way slowly down our driveway, a brilliant red male northern cardinal darted out from the hedge beside our house, followed the ambulance down the driveway, dove down toward it so the bird's feet just touched the roof, then swooped off into the sky again. It was almost as if the bird was "saluting" us. Mary never came to our earthly home again. It was her last ride down that driveway. And strangely, in the days that followed, I never noticed the cardinal anymore. It too seemed to be gone.

Mary and I accepted that bird's lovely song as simply a gift from God to encourage her days. So we'd remember that gift, I wanted a cardinal on her stone. It is there on the lower, left corner.

"All I Ever Wanted Was to Be a Mother"

I wanted the names of our children to be there too.

Mothering was central to who Mary was. I was reminded of that the first time I showed her mom the stone. It was Sunday, September 30, 2012. It would have been Mary's birthday. I had invited her mom and siblings over for lunch and to just "hang" together at my place, which is near the cemetery. After lunch I walked Mom over and we stood there for a while talking quietly, looking at the stone, remembering Mary. It was just the two of us for a short time.

I asked Mom to talk to me about what Mary was like as a young girl, before I knew her. I asked, "Mom, what do you remember about her when she was a young girl, say ten years old or less? What stands out to you? What was she like?" Mom thought for a minute, and said, "Oh Bert, she was such a little 'mother' even then."

It reminded me of something Mary said to me about a half year before she died. She was still doing very well then, but I remember a conversation we had about dreams. In case things didn't go the way we hoped, I had been thinking about whether Mary had really gotten what she wanted out of life. So I asked her if there was anything "unfinished?" Were there places she just wanted to go, were there things she wanted to do? Was there anything she had always dreamed of that she had not yet been able to do?

She said, "You know what hon? I didn't have that many dreams. All I ever really wanted was to be a mother." I told her I thought she was a great mother, a beautiful one! So to commemorate that, below our names, I had the names of our children etched: "Loving parents of Nathan, Adam, Sara and Aimee."

This is Not the End of Mary

Below that, along the bottom of the stone are some other significant words. The rest of the stone came to me fairly quickly. I knew exactly what I wanted it to say. But I struggled a long time over what to put along the bottom of the stone. I wanted words there that expressed our Christian hope. It is my Christian hope that sustains me in these days of grief, and it was her hope that sustained Mary in her death. So I wanted our stone to remind me, and to remind every person who sees it over the years that death is not the "end" of life, but a gateway to eternal life. I wanted to put words of scripture there, but words that would be unique.

After weeks of thinking and praying I had not found the verse I wanted.

And then I read I Thessalonians 5:10. It says, "He (Jesus) died for us so that, whether we are awake or asleep, we may live together with him." I read those words, then immediately read them again. In that instant, the words burned themselves on my memory. They were exactly the statement of hope I wanted to be there. So I added them along the bottom.

They were words of eternal hope. They strongly stated that this is not the end of Mary. This grave is not her resting place. It is the resting place of her body, and her body alone. She herself – the "person" of Mary – is not here, for she is alive together with Him. That's the single greatest comfort I have. And this verse so neatly summarizes that comfort.

How to Continue Living When Your Loved One is Gone

In the following weeks, I had three distinct encounters with the words of that verse. The first occurred about four weeks after I had commissioned our stone. It had not yet arrived. I was in the habit of stopping by the grave almost every day. It has become a favorite place for me to pray for a while. I was there one day, mid-evening. I was thinking about Mary, thanking God for many good memories. But I was also struggling very hard with grief that day. It was one of those times when the "waves" were pretty deep. I felt like they were dragging me under.

I was praying, telling God sometimes it just felt like I was merely existing, but no longer "living." I was telling Him it felt like I would never really "live" again. (By the way, I feel absolutely no guilt for praying that kind of prayer. I think the book of Job in the Bible is a huge invitation to us to honestly engage with God about what it feels like when life throws deeply hurtful things at us.) So there I was, telling God it didn't feel like I could ever live again. As I prayed, I thanked God for those words of hope He had given me. I thanked him for the words that would soon stand as a monument of hope over Mary's grave.

Suddenly some of those words came full-force to my attention. It was like God was nudging me by His Spirit to notice for the first time that they were not only words that reflected on Mary's condition. They spoke to my grieving condition too. They spoke to the very thing I had just been praying about.

"Whether we are *awake* or asleep, we may live," the verse stated. And I hadn't really noticed the *awake* part until now. "Awake means you," the Lord was reminding me. "Awake... you may live," He was pointing out to me. "You think maybe you can't 'live,' Bert? Yes you can 'live', Bert, yes you can." What an encouragement!

That was encounter number one with what this verse says. The words were becoming a richer stream of hope. I walked away from the grave with fresh hope not just for Mary, but for me. A second encounter came about twenty minutes later. I had left the grave site and was taking my evening power walk. As I walked, my cell phone rang, and it was my friend Len Thompson, from Edmonton. He wanted to know how I was doing, and I was telling him about my encounter with the verse, and how God was encouraging me to know I could actually "live" even after losing Mary.

As I walked, he began to discuss with me the whole concept of "life" in Biblical thinking. He had done a paper on it while working on his Master's Degree a few years before. He talked to me about the fact that the Ancient Hebrews didn't think of "life" quite the same as we do. In our thinking, a person is either "dead" or "alive." We tend to think in those two categories. We either have life or we don't. The Hebrews however, had a third category in their thinking about life and death. To them, a person could be "dead," could be "living-dead" or "alive." To be dead was to be gone from life. To be living-dead was to be alive, but not really alive. To be alive, was to be "fully alive," fully engaged in life.

That middle category, "living-dead" was to be in a condition where you body was functioning, you were biologically "alive," but your spirit was not functioning properly. So the Hebrew Psalms are full of language about living, but not being fully alive.

For example, in Psalm 6, David is in deep anguish of soul, feeling rebuked by God, disciplined, faint, in need of healing and deliverance (verses one to four). He has been talking about living "low" in life, then suddenly in verse five he is talking about death. "Among the dead no one proclaims your name, who praises you from the grave?" What Len was suggesting is that such language is probably not about actually dying biologically, but being "living-dead," in a place where your life has lost its passion and joy and hope and vitality.

David writes something similar in Psalm 31. In verse 10, he says his life "is consumed by anguish" and his years "by groaning." Poetically speaking, he is in a deeply sorrowful place, so much so, that it's as if he were "dead". He says in verse 12, "I am forgotten as though I were dead." It is probably that "living-dead" condition he is talking about.

In Psalm 30 he is celebrating the fact that he has been lifted from the depths. He writes, "Lord, my God, I called to you for help and you healed me. You, Lord, brought me up from the realm of the dead... (verses 2-3). He is probably not talking about a physical condition, being raised from biological death by God. He is referring to a heart condition. He says in verse 11, "You turned my wailing into dancing." He was alive in body but dead in spirit. But God brought his spirit back to life. He was "living-dead", but now he is once more "living-alive."

That three-category thinking is part of New Testament language too. So Jesus says things like, "I have come that they may have life, and have it *to the full*" (John 10:10, emphasis mine). And Paul, knowing full well we live in a world where death and hurt are common to us all, says, "Rejoice in the Lord always. I will say it again: Rejoice! (i.e., live like you are alive! Philippians 4:4).

What Len was suggesting came into my heart like another encounter with that verse I was going to put on the stone. It says, whether awake or asleep, "we may live" together with Him. Len was saying it probably was not meant to tell me, or anyone else who came to visit the grave, "you can go on," or "you can continue to exist," or "you can function in body, but not function in your spirit, living a low level of life, filled with depression and self-pity and sadness." No, this was God saying again what He said in Jesus, "you can live, really live!" This was God reminding me I can actually "rejoice always," even without Mary to walk with.

A Third Encounter

A third encounter with those words on Mary's stone was a little slower in coming--two months later, Wednesday, September 17. By now the words had come to mean so much to me. The stone itself would not arrive for a few days, but I would often think of what was going to be written there. I was very encouraged by the first two encounters with the words. Mary was really "alive", and I could "really" live here on earth, in spite of my wife being in heaven.

But something was a little disquieting for me. To receive a promise like that is one thing, but to live it is another. I was fumbling a bit for the "how" of what the verse said. Not for Mary. I knew about that "how." She is alive with God, as the verse says, because "he (Christ) died for us." But the "how" for me felt much less finished.

How was I supposed to "really live?" Was I supposed to grit my teeth and do it? Was I just supposed to "pretend," to just tell everyone how great I was doing until they believed it and I actually began to believe it myself? Was I supposed to pray long enough and hard enough to kind of "forget" my sorrow, almost like I was "medicating" myself with faith, using it as an escape from pain? Was I supposed to just keep busy enough to keep the hurt from overwhelming me? Were any of those the "path" toward being really "alive?" They didn't feel like it. They felt more like a path to "living-dead."

I was standing at the grave, praying about it again, telling God I wanted to do what that verse said. I wanted to be "alive," impossible as it felt, but wasn't sure how to do it.

Then the last phrase of the verse suddenly came to my conscious mind. It was, "whether we are awake or asleep, we may live *together with Him*." That last phrase, I suddenly realized, was hinting about a path. It was talking to me about a way. It was not only "what" was true of Mary and "could" be true of me, it was telling me *how* it could be true of me. I could live, really live, if I lived "together with" Him.

A New and Living Way

So what does it mean to live together with Jesus? I read a commentary that pointed out that the words "live together with him," could be rendered, "to live in fellowship with him." Just as the highest description of our eternal life is to live in fellowship and proximity to God, so the highest path of our current life is to live in close fellowship with Him. It is to simply walk with Him through my moments and my days, whatever they bring.

So I've been working on living out what that means. Here's what it looks like for me right now. It is different from walking in fellowship with another person. He is Spirit, not body. I can't actually touch Him, hold His hand or audibly speak with Him. But my walking in fellowship with Him is still something that is to be done in my body.

So here's how I'm trying to do it. I wake up and a song of praise is often running through my mind. Just before I go to sleep, I often ask God to wake me up with a song. I wake up, go to the bathroom, and I'm thinking about the song as I shower. I think about the song, and let it run through my mind as I make breakfast. As I eat, I open my Bible to do my daily readings. As I do that, I consciously try to do it "with" Him. I listen for what he may be trying to communicate to me today. I write it down in my devotional journal. I pray about it.

I also write it on a little notepad I carry around in my shirt pocket. Throughout the day, as I get a minute, during work breaks, I pull out what I have written down. I think about it, and I pray about it some more.

Things happen at work. I get stuck on things in trailer design (my job). When I feel my mind bogging down on a challenge, I stop to pray again. I ask God to show me a way to do things, and then I run for a few minutes with whatever comes to mind. I draw a bit then stop to analyze. Often I've come up with something "new" that looks like it's worth developing. When that happens I breathe a "Thank you," and carry on with it. Other times not too much "new" comes, but I'm given mental strength to keep "pushing" at what's in front of me. I give thanks for that too.

At noon I often walk a bit to stretch my legs because I sit way too much. As I walk, I think and pray. I take the slow way home, Old Simcoe Street. It gives me a chance to sip some green tea as I drive, to think, to pray some more. I get the mail, make supper, clean up, and then most days, I take a long walk. I usually stop first at Mary's grave. It really is my favorite place to pray, mostly prayers of gratitude to God for the life he gave us together.

As I walk, I think and pray about all kinds of stuff. I don't try to get words "right." I just talk to him about work and family and extended family and just "life". Sometimes the prayers are not really "conscious" or "verbal." Sometimes I'm just thinking about things, but I'm conscious that I'm thinking them "before him." I walk for a little over an hour.

The Path Feels Right

That's a brief picture of what I think "together with Him" looks like. I don't want to seem as if I've "arrived". That's not it at all. I often get distracted. I find myself not thinking of Him at all and sometimes just feel too busy or too tired to talk to Him. It takes energy.

But here's what I am discovering about living together with Jesus. I can keep pulling myself back to fellowship with Him. It's a path that keeps inviting me back. He keeps inviting me back. I'm finding it enlivens my inner man. And it is feeling more and more like life, real life. It feels like the right path.

Do I still miss Mary? Absolutely and completely. Do I wish I could walk and talk with her? Of course I do! But walking this valley with the Lord, I am finding a new joy starting to be born in my soul. As I write this, it is early Sunday morning, Thanksgiving weekend. I get to worship with God's people, and I still have so much to be thankful for. I'm thankful Mary is "alive," and thankful that I can "live." Thank You, God!

The stone is really my last gift to Mary. I know if she could see it, she would be thrilled with every part of it. She'd take my hand again, capture me again with those deep blue eyes of hers, and say, "Thanks hon, it's beautiful." Then she'd seal it with a kiss and one of her special hugs.

REFLECTION

1. If I could sit beside you, as your Dad (or brother or grandpa or friend), I think I'd want to ask you about your stone. I'd want to do that, for the day is surely coming when you too will need a

stone. And I think I'd want to lovingly ask you, "What would someone who really KNOWS you and really LOVES you want to put on your stone?"

2. How did you react to the cardinal story? How could it be, or could it not be a God-thing?

3. I talk about the phrase "together with Him" pointing us to a path toward real life. Can you think of any other Scriptures that would confirm this to be the right path?

4. How does a person get on that path and how do we stay on that path?

5. Why is that an important question to be able to answer?

Epilogue

The longer I lived with Mary, and the longer I am without her, the more I feel that she was a gift. She was a beautiful gift. And it often feels so very alone to be without her. "Missing her" doesn't even begin to describe the feeling.

I was a little overwhelmed with that feeling on July 8, 2013. That morning, in my devotional reading I came to Psalm 131. The Psalm reads as follows:

> 1. *"My heart is not proud, Lord,*
>
> *My eyes are not haughty;*
>
> *I do not concern myself with great matters*
>
> *Or things too wonderful for me.*
>
> 2. *But I have calmed and quieted myself,*
>
> *I am like a weaned child with its mother;*
>
> *Like a weaned child, I am content.*
>
> 3. *Israel, put your hope in the Lord*
>
> *Both now and forevermore.*

It got me thinking about where I was and how I could move forward from here. The first verse warns me about pride: being too self-centered. That, it seemed to say, would take me in a direction opposite to where I wanted to go, asking endless questions with no answers. Instead of pride, the Psalm in verse two urges me to calm and quiet myself like a weaned child with its mother. A weaned child, it seems, is content. A child not yet weaned is by contrast, not content.

Reading that made my mind drift back to the time when Mary was breast-feeding our babies. I do remember the "discontent" talked about here. When they were being breast-fed, the babies were not being content with Mary. All they wanted was what she was giving them. And just about all they wanted was more of it. I would tell Mary how beautiful it was to me to see her feeding our baby. She would usually find it beautiful too, but sometimes she would say to me, "It might look beautiful to you, but sometimes it makes me feel like I'm nothing but a breast. It's all this kid wants from me."

That's the way it is with an un-weaned child. Comfort, companionship, love and a host of other important things that flow from a mother-child relationship don't have any place in an un-weaned mind. The un-weaned mind is rarely just content when with its mother. That mind is on one track only, and thinks of Mom as having one purpose only. Give me what I want. Give me what I need. And give it to me now!

A weaned child however, begins to see a lot more in its mother. She becomes more and more a full-orbed person to the weaned mind. To her weaned children, Mary became so much more than a nurturing breast.

She became companion and teacher and a person of comfort and encouragement. Her lap became the favorite place to just "be" for a while. It was a space in which they loved to sit and snuggle. Her children loved to just sit there while she held them and sang songs over them or read a story to them. Her lap became a place to rest. It became probably the most contented place on earth for them.

Somehow, that is to be a picture, even now, of how it is with my soul and my God. My un-weaned soul cries out to God only for what He gives to me. Comfort me! I want...! I need....!

While I think it's okay to have those moments and conversations with God, and to express my needs to Him, I don't think I am meant to stay there very long. This Psalm invites me past that. It invites me to go further.

God wants me to be weaned. He wants me to come to him for companionship and teaching, and to be willing to just spend time "on His lap". He wants me to rest there and to hear the stories He longs to read over me.

Because of that, though I miss Mary, in my privileged place on His lap, I am never alone. There I am learning to listen to His story. My prayer is that you, my readers, would do the same.

Walk with Him,

Bert.

Acknowledgements

To our sons and daughters, Nathan and Jennifer, Adam, Sara, Aimee and Christopher: you were often in my thoughts as I wrote. These words are first of all for you, a remembering of Mom's love-walk, something I pray you will cherish and emulate. Your Mom knew how to love us. I hope you always remember that. I am thankful for every one of you.

To our grandchildren, Noah and Joel: I hope that these words about Grandma will be a special legacy for you. Our family is missing a lot without Grandma. But we still have a lot too.

To Mom: you passed on to your daughter so many lessons on how to love her husband and family. I hope you will always be proud of Mary. She learned those lessons well.

To our extended family: you have fueled my desire to finish writing. You were always so precious to Mary. The love between sisters is an especially beautiful thing and I wanted her life-lessons to be put into words for you.

Len, our conversations in my time of sorrow were seminal. You helped me clarify many of my thoughts. You were a sounding-board for many of my tentative God-thoughts. Thank you for being the faithful, loyal and wise friend you are, and for making time to interact with my words when you were in the middle of the busiest season of your life.

So many people have continued to pray for me in this year of loss. I often felt I was being carried along by your prayers. Being carried by someone else's prayers is not just an idea. It is a reality. To say "Thank you," hardly seems like enough.

To the Small Group at Calvary Baptist Church, of which Mary and I were privileged to be a part: John and Natalie, Arnold and Mary-Anne, Chris and Julia, Terry and Debbie, John and Gail: you have been a small group from heaven, a gift of God to Mary and me. You walked our cancer journey with us, and I am so grateful. So often, you guys were Jesus to us. Words fail me.

To my editor, Emily Wierenga: You get it. I was afraid at first to have someone else interact with my words as an editor must. But you get it. You understand when a person's heart experiences pain and deep things. I never get the feeling I am fighting with you over my words. Instead you get inside the words, understand them, and then improve them. You have sharpened my words and I owe you a debt of gratitude. You have been a true friend to my words, and an encouragement to my spirit. Thank you too for your prayers.

To my friends at Prodigal Press: As I participated in your program for first-time authors, you consistently hammered home the message that writing is as much work as it is inspiration. You have encouraged me to just sit down and get it done. You have shown me the value of re-writing and re-writing. I have learned a lot from the things you have shared with the whole class. Thank you for being willing to work with first-timers. Many publishers can't be bothered. You have shared prodigally. You have lived up to your name. Many thanks.

Father, God: There are weaknesses in both who I am and what I write. For those I accept present blame, thankful that it is not eternal. There are also glimpses of light and truth which you have gently but firmly worked into my soul. Mary no longer holds my hand, but you still hold my heart. Thank You, Lord.